DELIGHT OF THE OVERCLASS!

DEMISE OF THE MIDDLECLASS!

DELIGHT OF THE OVERCLASS!

DEMISE OF THE MIDDLECLASS!

JAY T. BALDWIN

ISBN: 1-58820-490-1

1stBooks – rev. 11/13/00

CONTENTS

Dedicated with love to my beautiful daughter
Adriana and to all of the children
and the future of America.

Chapter 1 A peek at the adversary, the richest of the rich..

Overclass! This is a relatively new term. It makes every hair on my head stand on end. It sounds like a term depicting a ruthless, over-bearing elite in a George Orwell novel, or some other science fiction book.

In 1984 Newsweek Magazine addressed the birth of a new species of successful Americans. This new comer was nick named "The Yuppie". Jerry Adler, in his article "OVERCLASS, How the new elite scrambled up the merit ladder-and wants to stay there any way it can." He quotes, "you've probably never heard of the overclass, which is just how it's members like it; they have a lot to answer for. They are the people who put Jim Carrey on magazine covers, who renamed blue-green "teal" and keep loaning money to Donald Trump - not out of any sinister conspiracy to ruin the country but because, well, it's their job. As "professionals" and "managers" they lay claim to an increasing share of the national income, but they wind up spending most of it at mirror-walled restaurants where they have to eat $10 arugla salads."

"Choking the chicken!" Americans feeling the financial strangle hold tighten, as the overclass help themselves to an increasing portion of the national income. As this overclass stakes claim to a larger slice of the American Dream pie, this ultimately means smaller portions, and lower standard of living for the rest of us.

[Illustration 1]

This overclass constitutes of about 12.5 million people with incomes starting at $114,000 a year. This is a scant 5% of the entire population of the United States. Fifteen years ago, we would have never thought this handful of Yuppies, upper-class, overclass or whatever could incubate the ugliest lesion to fester on the American dream of the other 95%. Now we are witnessing capitalism at its utmost greediest extreme.

Let's take a good look at this new growing terror that has raised its ugly head to the American dream. I will briefly describe this ominous serpent. Have you ever heard of "in your face capitalism"?

Since the beginning in a capitalistic society, there have been class stratification. Some people are wealthier than others, some are poorer. Corporations and businesses have scrambled to keep costs down and production up.

There have always been employee hiring's and firing's. I can't forget the biggest goal of all capitalist's - "profit" – and to get as much of it as possible.

This is the American way. It's as American as apple pie and Chevrolet! However, today these wonderfully successful ingredients have recombined in the witch's brewing pot to create one of the most dangerous sharks to infest the seas of American society and lifestyle. Here is an example. You and you're co-workers are forced to accept a sizable pay cut and benefit reduction. Some of you may get fired, or laid off! Then suddenly your company's stock prices skyrocket, profits go ballistic, and your already wealthy CEO gives himself a big fat raise. You can probably bet another Rolls Royce, another vacation home somewhere, and maybe a new yacht!

There was a time not to many years ago, if you gave pay cuts and laid employees off, it was considered shameful. It meant you f - - ed up! However, today your stock prices soar, the CEO's wallet gets fatter, and the champagne corks fly at Wall Street!

This "in you're face capitalism" is an equal opportunity shark. Regardless if you are black, white, red, yellow, male, female, educated or non-educated, we all stand a good chance of being the next bucket of fish heads over the stern.

Let's see what a few wealthy have said and done to raise profit margins, stock prices, and eventually, their own pay. Here is a good one: "Villains? Heck, no. We're like doctors. Job cuts hurt, but it keeps firms alive", says Albert Dunlop, former CEO of Scott Paper. He is known as "Chainsaw Al", after cutting 11,000 jobs in 1994. After merging his company with the Kimberly Clark company, he soaked up a cool million in stocks, profits, personal salary raises, and other fringe benefits. He also downsized seven of his other companies. To name a couple, Diamond International and Lily Tulip. I wonder where he found a rubber band big enough to wrap around that wad of cash?

Robert Allen, CEO of AT&T, dialed up a salary of $3,362,000 as he disconnected 40,000 workers in January 1996.

Walter Shipley of Chemical/Chase Manhattan, with a juicy salary of $2,496,154 as of August 1995, canceled 12,000 paychecks.

Louis Gerstner, CEO of IBM, with an eye watering salary of $2,625,000, laid off an ungodly 60,000 workers in July 1993.

Charles Lee CEO of GTE Corporation has a dream tingling $2,004,115 salary after 17,000 layoffs in January 1994.

John McDonnell chairman of McDonnell Douglas Aircraft Corporation with a wide body $577,791, power stalled 17,000 workers.

Ronald Allen, CEO of Delta Airlines, seated a comfortable $475,000 income as he booked 15,000 employees on a one-way flight out of the company in April 1994.

Robert Stemple, former CEO of General Motors Corporation, with a Cadillac Fleetwood sized paycheck of $1,000,000, test crashed a whopping 74,000 layoffs in December 1991.

Edward Brennan, former CEO of Sears Roebuck and Company, with a rosy annual income of $3,075,000, fed 50,000 employees to the sharks in January 1993.

Robert Palmer, CEO of Digital Equipment, had a nice salary program of $900,000 as he deleted 20,000 workers in May 1994.

Michael Miles, former CEO of Philip Morris, made a sweet smelling $1,000,000 income, as he bagged 14,000 layoffs in November 1993.

Frank Shrontz, CEO of Boeing Aircraft Corporation, with a wing buffeting Salary of $1,420,934, tail-spinned 28,000 workers into the ground in February 1993.

William Ferguson, former CEO of Nynex Corporation, punched up an $800,000 income as he cleared 16,800 employees in January 1994.

Shall I keep going? Here is what one egotistical, greedy CEO Bob Allen said when confronted by Newsweek in January 1996. "He felt bad about firing people but saw no point in giving up some of his pay or perks as a shared sacrifice with his workers. And, he said, he saw no reason to apologize: 'I wouldn't see any value of going on TV and crying.'" Allen was strongly criticized on Wall Street for AT&T's $7.5 billion hostile takeover of computer maker NCR in 1991. He pocketed more than $5 million when his stocks and options skyrocketed after the layoffs were announced.

During a large merger between Chase Manhattan and Chemical Bank, 12,000 jobs were cancelled. Ironically, all those people were laid-off to enable the company to pay it's new CEO Gilbert Amelio $2,500,000 in annual salaries.

Jill Smolowe, in her article, "Reap As Ye Shall Sow", Time Magazine February 5, 1996, hits the nail on the head. "Pay-for-performance standards are a jackpot this year for executives, but not for workers." In her article these greedy CEOs are even reaping the extra earnings meant for the stock investors. She quotes: "Angry investors close out the Decade of Greed with the demands that executive compensation be tied to company performance. In other words, CEOs should pocket a bundle only if they make a bundle. And make a bundle they did. By laying off employees, merging and acquiring at a record pace, slicing employee health care costs and scoring strong sales, U.S. companies enjoyed record profits in 1995." Now CEOs are reaping what stock holders sowed. Results, as published in corporate proxy statements, are just starting to roll in, but it is already clear the gold rush is on." This kind of defines having you're pie and eating it too!!!!

It's plain and obvious as the nose on you're face, this "in you're face capitalism" shark has an insatiable appetite, but shows no signs of sharing.

Ms. Smolowe's article goes on to explain how the second largest merger in U.S. history, between Capitol Cities/ABC and Walt Disney, netted the Magic Kingdom's Micheal Eisner a giant mouse sized $14.8 million compensation package. This was a magic 40% increase in his annual pay-check. This single man commanded a cosmic $19 billion merger. Absolutely mind boggling isn't it? She also goes on to say how David Johnson, chairman of Campbell Soup took home a thick and hearty, delicious $6.6 million. This guy gave himself a galactic 150% pay raise, as his stocks soared 36% to 60. Donald Beall, of Rockwell International, also took home a Rocky Mountain sized $5.5 million pay check, after his stocks launched up almost 50%, a nice 45% pay increase from his 1994 income. Charles Walgreen, of the Walgreen drug store chain, wrote himself a prescription for an 82% personal income fix to $4 million annually as his stocks checked out up 37% for the year.

Smolowe quotes; "On Wall street where the M and A frenzy made for a historic $458 billion worth of deals-up from the previous high of $347 billion just 12 months earlier, compensation experts are calculating that several CEOs banked more than $3 million. To wit: despite the gush of profits, stockholders didn't see a comparable leap in their dividends.

And employees took home only 2.7% more in wages and benefits during the year, the lowest increase since the government began tracking compensation in '81. As the compensation gap grows, so does the pain gap. At a time when Americans are paying higher health insurance premiums for more restricted services, CEOs of health-maintenance organizations, who ordain who shall be treated and who shall not, are banking pay checks far more than double the average CEO compensation in other companies of comparable size and performance. A prime example: Daniel Crowly, CEO of Foundation Health Corp., a California based HMO. According to one expert, Crowly's average annual compensation for the past three years was $6.1 million, besting his counterparts in other industries by 277%. Though turn-of-the-century financier J.P. Morgan argued that a CEO should never make more than 20 times the average salary of a company's employees, the ratio has escalated radically in recent years. In a sample of 292 Fortune 500 companies, the ratio was 143 to 1 in 1992 and now is approaching 185 to 1." What the Sam hell is going on here???? It is clearly evident that these boys aren't taking Mr. Morgan's (the most successful business man in the world) business advice, and weren't taught to share by their mothers!!! Possibly some of these guys were problem children when they were young. This was just a list of some of the household names.

With the epochal birth of this new super-breed, this greedier class, we are watching the life force literally being drained out of America. **This out right rape of a nation has to stop!** Yet, we're still wondering why our pay checks are getting smaller, our standard of living is declining and the rich are getting richer, and the poor are getting poorer. You know the saying "You have to rob Peter to pay Paul!"

This doesn't even begin to show the thousands of smaller less known corporations who are practicing "in you're face capitalism". The American Management Association surveyed companies in July 1995. Over29% were expected to cut salaries and lay-off workers in a twelve month period of time. The A.M.A. thinks the actual figure may be closer to 60%.

Through my own Personal experience, comments and experiences from family, friends and co-workers, I have learned of many other ways corporations of all sizes practice "in you're face capitalism". Here are just a few examples. Some corporations practice, what I have coined the ninety day wonder approach to staffing their work force. They will hire a worker or workers for jobs requiring little training, then keep them for just under 90 days and fire them. The reasons for termination are usually false, or on a small error not usually severe enough to warrant termination on the employee's part. I have been a victim of this ploy more than once. It's ironic these same firms run ads in the classified section of the local news papers 52 weeks of the year for the same positions. I assume they do this to avoid paying benefits, sick days, holidays and paid vacations, and most of all, pay raises. They usually keep stacks of employment applications ready to roll. Next victim please!!!

Here is another more subtle approach. The company will hire employees on an hourly basis, later on switching them over to a commission or percentage of work done. When the employees are transferred to the new compensation plan, their weekly pay usually decreases and the hours and responsibilities are greatly increased. The end result is you end up working sometimes double the hours and twice as hard for a heck of a lot less money. I have been a victim of this one also.

I don' t know exactly how, but some corporations have ways around the state and federal overtime laws. These corporations will work employees more than 40 hours a week and still only pay them their normal hourly pay. Some times the workers work 7 days a week and put in more than 70 hours a week. I have been in this circumstance more than once. I thought the federal overtime laws dictates all employees must receive time and a half after 40 hours a week????

Here is another sneaky "in your face" violation of federal overtime laws. A company will work it's employees past the 40 hour limit, as the hours increase above the 40th hour, the amount per hour decreases proportionately from the normal hourly rate. In this sweet deal, if one works enough hours, he ends up working for merely pennies an hour. The slang name for this cute deal is called Chinese overtime. No offense meant to my Asian readers!

One of the most increasingly common methods companies employ to avoid paying benefits, holidays, sick days, paid vacations and raises, is to hire only part time staffs dividing the day into two shifts or hire from a temporary employment firm.

I have been on many interviews and been employed by at least 12 different firms in the past 7 years. I have seen all of these techniques used, sometimes in combinations. One common element used is for the corporations to round all hours and dollars to the company's benefit. All or most of these techniques are clearly unethical and are in violation of state and federal labor laws. If any of these violations were to be challenged by one single employee he/she will probably be terminated and / or silenced. Only by uniting with fellow co-workers for the same cause and filing a free joint or class action complaint with the Dept. of Labor will the workers be successful and minimize risks to their jobs.

I have looked employers, and potential employers in the eyes asking how am supposed to support my family on these meager wages and little or no benefits. Some of the responses were as follows: "That's not my problem!" "That seems to be you're problem!" "I am not running a social program here!" "That is all we can pay!", or a whole host of other smart cocky remarks and answers to that question.

It is clearly obvious these corporate big shots spend thousands of dollars in legal fees creating new innovative ways to shaft the American worker. Deregulation of corporate America has given businesses too much freedom. Now they are utilizing every method and loophole in the existing labor regulatory structure to fatten their profits at our expense. Who knows how many other methods are being utilized out there.

Bend over baby!!!! By the way, you will have to bring your own Vaseline!!

[**Illustration 2**]

All Hee Hawed Out! The harder you work, the less you earn.

ALL HEE HAWED OUT! One would think the harder you work, the more reward you're entitled too. That's not always the case! Some companies will pay their employees a fixed salary, then a percentage commission after a production quota is reached. However, when the quota is reached, it is then raised. This means a pay cut for the worker. Ex. $300 is the base salary, once the production goal is achieved, a 10% commission bonus is paid. The weekly production quota is $5000. Two or three weeks running, the employee works real hard, and the quota is surpassed by $400. So the employee has maintained a $5400 in production. He is then earning $300 base salary, plus $40 in commission which is 10% of $400. That's $340 a week. Management then raises his production quota to $5400 a week. Now the employee is back to earning only $300 a week. This forces the employee to work even harder to regain the extra income. Now, the employee has to work $5800 in production to again earn $340 a week. This cycle is then repeated again and again. Eventually, the worker is doing $6000+ in production quotas and is only earning $300 a week, because it is humanly impossible to surpass the final quota. In my case, I ended up earning less, after many months with the company, than I did when I first started. Yet my production had doubled and I was working almost double the hours in a vain effort to make more than $300 a week. The only one benefiting here, is the boss!!! Is that human exploitation or What? Makes you feel like a beast of burden! **The lesson here is not to surpass you're production goal too many weeks in a row, but only occasionally, no matter how tempting the extra income can be.** We, the people of America, must not allow this exploitation to continue. <u>Do not fall into the same trap as I did!!!!</u>

DEMISE OF THE MIDDLECLASS

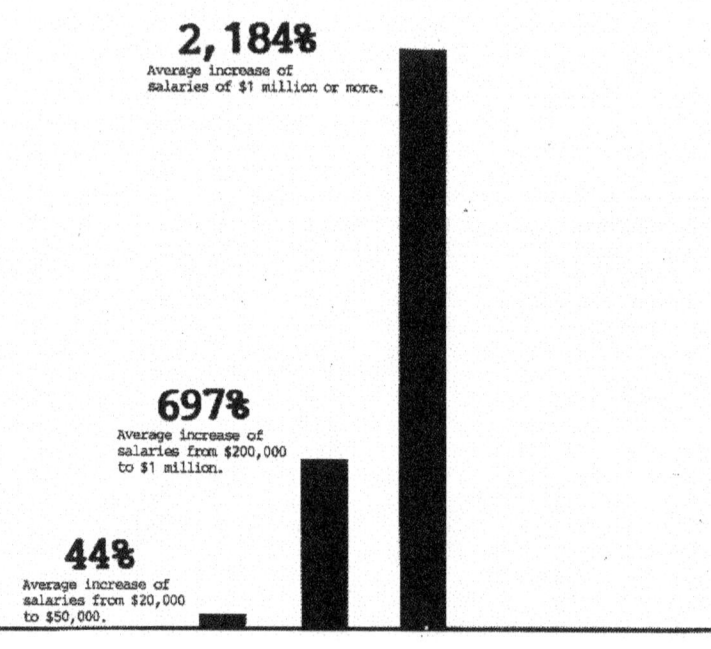

2,184%
Average increase of
salaries of $1 million or more.

697%
Average increase of
salaries from $200,000
to $1 million.

44%
Average increase of
salaries from $20,000
to $50,000.

Demise of the Middleclass as we once knew it! The Internal Revenue Service figures and the results of corporate deregulation in the decade of the 1980's. Ironically, this has resulted in a 2,184% increase in the salaries of the overclass, the largest increase in the salaries of the overclass, the largest increase of the richest incomes in recorded history. However, the middleclass has had only a 44% increase in the same period of time. If a family earning $13,000 a year at poverty level, had the same increase in their income as the rich, they would have an unbelievable $283,920 annual income! Poverty would no longer exist! This is the beginning of the end of our middleclass culture. Is a class war inevitable??

[Illustration 3]

12

Chapter 2 Delight of the overclass. The rich are getting richer

One would think that society, especially in a democracy where the majority rule, would not tolerate the smallest minority of its population exploiting the rest for it's financial and social gain. However, today not much seems to be being done to prevent this.

Now that we know a little about the adversary, let's see how fat our money hungry shark is getting. Oops! I think we will need the flight deck of the U.S.S. Enterprise to lay this one out on!

In Time magazine, February 19, 1996, Jane Bryant Quinn says it like it is in, in her article "A Paycheck Revolt in '96?", "Without a question, it's a great time to be rich. Still, millions of people are working harder for less reward. Real earnings are flat down. The chasm between the rich and poor is the widest since 1947 (that's as far back as the numbers go)." Don' t you think this can qualify as a serious national dilemma?

Consulting all of my sources, I will try to put some fairly accurate numbers on this monumental problem. In 1972 some 24.1% of all of the nation's assets, real estate, stocks and bonds, insurance and household goods etc, were owned by the richest 1% of the population. This is the wealthiest of the rich 5% of the population. That was high enough then! Hold on to you're seat! Let's see how today's figures stack up. By 1992, the wealthiest 1 % of the entire population now controls a staggering 42% of the nations gross assets such as real estate, stocks and bonds insurances and household items, and a whopping 50% of all financial assets. I can only imagine what the remaining 4% of this overclass controls. By 1992, the richest 1% had an explosive 91% increase in personal income. The remaining 4% of this elite had a staggering 28% leap in personal income levels. These 1992 figures are probably much larger now.

Like a giant cosmic black hole, just listen to that giant sucking sound, this overclass is literally gobbling up our hopes, dreams, standards of living, quality of life and our entire nation!!!!

Here is some more food for thought. This greedy elite is socking over 15% of their incomes into savings. While the unfortunate middleclass is scraping a mere 2.1% of it's income into the piggy bank. This is down from roughly 3 - 4% not too many years ago. Some middleclass incomes have barely stood their ground, but most cases have fallen. The average American income for college graduates has fallen 11%. income for high school graduates has taken a 16% dive. By my personal experience here in South Florida, that figure is closer to 50%. Income for high school dropouts has plummeted 28% from 1979 to 1994. The poorest 5% of the population known as the underclass, helplessly watched it's personal income take a disheartening 17% dive. **What in God's name is going on here???**

This ungodly, unfair distribution of financial and national assets is at an all time 63 year high.

In the lap of luxury. Today's elite have wealth and power beyond your wildest dreams. The overclass of today is by far wealthier, and is earning well over 150 times the income of their wealthy peers 15-20 years ago. The predictions indicate they have only just begun, and will attain unlimited wealth in the future. However, today's working middleclass is only earning, an estimated, 1-2 times the salary of their forerunners of 20 years ago. This doesn't take into account the cost of living has more than quadrupled in the same period. The rich are getting richer, the middle-class and poor are getting poorer!

[Illustration 4]

[Illustration 5]

New Deal - Fair Deal = Raw Deal!
(see illustration 5)

Under the New Deal, employees have kept their end of the bargain by increasing production, sharpening skills, developing new ones, contributing more time and responsibility at the work place. They are working harder than ever before! Diane E. Lewis of The Boston Globe says 94% of all employees agree it's their responsibility to work harder and more diligently contributing more to the firm, if they plan on keeping their jobs. Ironically, even with record corporate profits and skyrocketing executive salaries, the bosses are not keeping their end of the deal by not sharing the financial spoils with the workers. Trickle Down Theory? This thing ain't leaking a drop!! In April 1996, Business Week reported executive pay soared an unbelievable 27%. White collar workers gained a mere 1.2%, and blue collar workers suffered a sickening 2% decline. This decade long trend is eroding all faith in management in the eyes of the American workers. I think it is about time to give these corporate gluttons a dose of their own medicine!

This definitely defines being taken to the cleaners. However, corporate America has brain washed all of us almost on a daily basis by crying crocodile tears, claiming the economy is so bad, there is too much competition, expenses and salaries are draining the company or some other lame excuse to warrant all of their cut backs. Anybody with half a brain who has done a little research on these mega corporations, will realize the real truth. It seems that the CEOs and the upper management of America's largest corporations do not want to see their own lavish incomes stagnate. Like a glutton, they expect continual raises, and by no means

WAGE PLUNGE

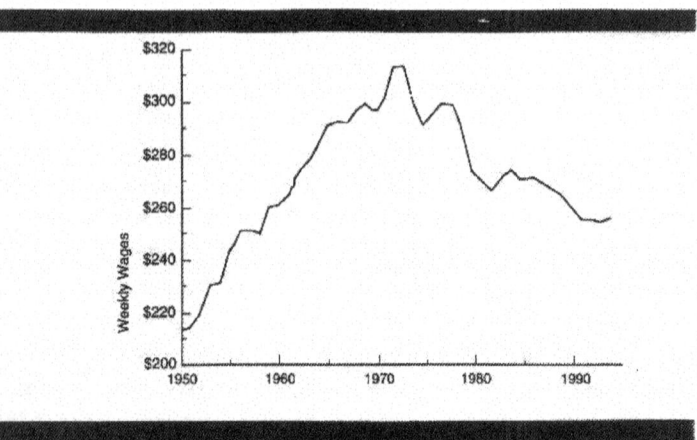

Falling like a rock! Inflation adjusted wages plunge, unless you are a member of the overclass. Almost on a daily basis, we hear how good the economy is doing. How corporate profits of America's larger companies have reaped record profits. Unemployment is at an all time low. Executive and CEO pay has increased two thousand fold. Wonder what planet this is occurring on? For every one out in the working class, we might as well be on another planet! The richest fifth has seen the greatest increase in annual income in the history of the entire developed free world, yet the average American is now earning inflation adjusted wages back to that of 1960. In a world where the cost of living is five times that of 1969, just to live the quality of life of 1969, we now have to have four full time jobs per family. It seems America has a double standard economy. One for the rich! One for everyone else!

[Illustration 6]

18

wouldn't even think about a pay cut with their loyal employees.

Do you feel like crying yet? Unfortunately, today our capitalistic system is more geared than ever before to thrust this wealthy, rich and powerful elite up the socio-economic ladder. Unfortunately, today small business, the middleclass and the poor are footing the bill. Yet amidst shrinking incomes, sliding standards of living, society searches for scapegoats trying unsuccessfully to treat the symptoms. Still we sit back and wonder why bankruptcies, bad credit, hunger, home foreclosures, evictions and the homeless are on the increase, breaking the back of the American welfare system. As a society we seem to look the other way and refuse to recognize the real culprits, the true guilty party, the overclass.

As you will discover in succeeding chapters, the need for increased government regulation of corporate America. Then you will see a definite need of policing these governmental regulatory agencies to ensure they are not succumbing to corruption and bribery. There is growing discontentment in the current system, and we are facing a very serious threat to our free and Democratic society if this problem goes ignored.

You'll learn how this powerful corporate elite uses it's juggernaut powers to mold and manipulate personal as well as societal values to benefit them and how most laws are designed to appease them.

How throughout history an exploited, down-trodden majority end up

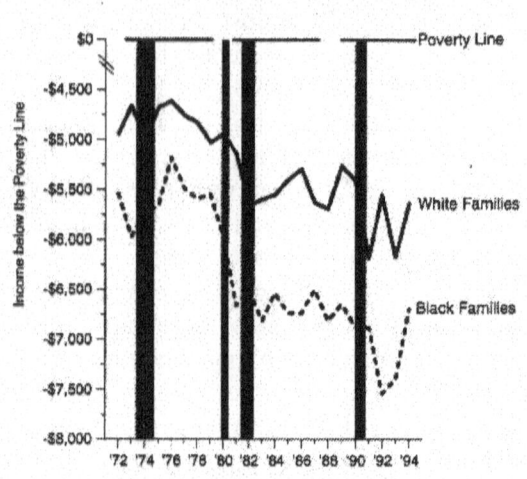

The poor are getting poorer! Families of all races and nationalities are suffering the same fate. Is this the indications of a serious social problem, or is this just our imagination????

[Illustration 7]

electing an enemy counter democratic political power as a last ditch effort to eliminate their suffering and how this threat exists for America. There could be a real possibility, as the masses are backed into a no win financial corner, of a violent civil upheaval and maybe a second civil war unless the middleclass and poor unite immediately!

20

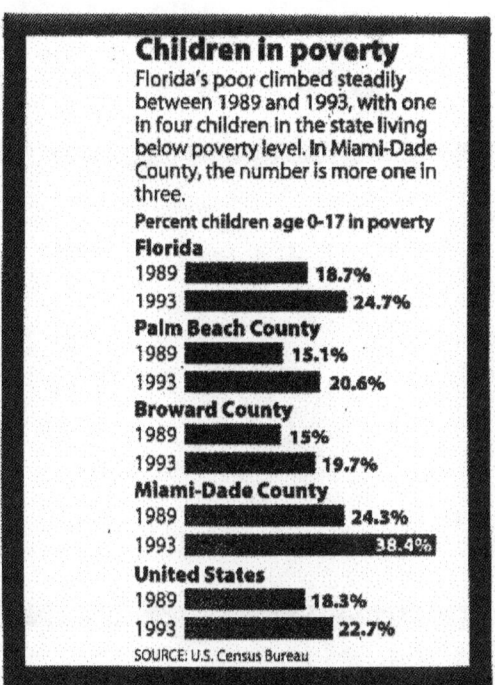

Children in poverty

Florida's poor climbed steadily between 1989 and 1993, with one in four children in the state living below poverty level. In Miami-Dade County, the number is more one in three.

Percent children age 0-17 in poverty

Florida
1989 — 18.7%
1993 — 24.7%

Palm Beach County
1989 — 15.1%
1993 — 20.6%

Broward County
1989 — 15%
1993 — 19.7%

Miami-Dade County
1989 — 24.3%
1993 — 38.4%

United States
1989 — 18.3%
1993 — 22.7%

SOURCE: U.S. Census Bureau

Children in poverty. Children growing up in poor families is on a rapid increase not just in Florida, but the entire nation. According to the U.S. Census Bureau, the percentage of children ages 0 – 17, nationwide, has increased 4.4% in four years from 1989 to 1993. These are the most recent years done in the census. These figures are, more than likely, much higher now in 1998, as more families continue to slide below the poverty level due to diminishing after tax incomes, and/or diminishing purchasing power because of increasing inflation.

[Illustration 8]

21

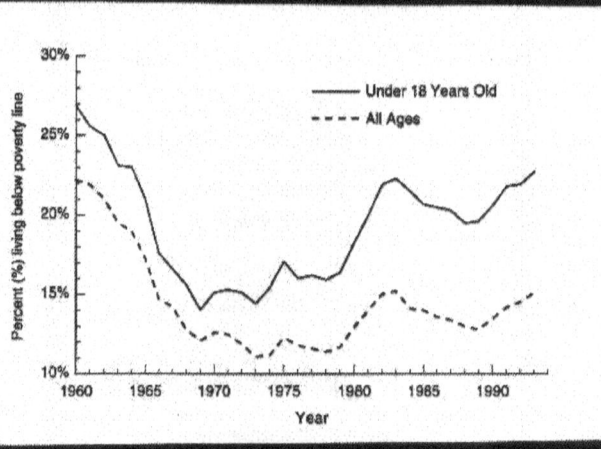

The gradual incline. Since 1969, the poverty rate has risen much more than it has fallen. One will notice a ten year cycle, where in 1969, 1979 and again in 1989, the percentage of poor took a giant leap upward. Each time the incline was a little steeper, and lasted a little longer, only to never return to previous year levels.

[Illustration 9]

Chapter 3 The wealthy deal the cards. Money is power.

In all societies, through out history, there have been some form of socio-economic classes, levels or stratification of the people. Some classes have more while some have less. America's capitalistic system is no exception. This raises the biggest question sociologists ask themselves, who benefits from the existing social order and status quo and who doesn't? One editorial writer asks; "Must we continue to concentrate power and wealth in the hands of the few, preserving income gaps that have virtually remained undisturbed through the New Deal, Fair Deal, New Frontier, and Great Society - or is there a better way? Must millions of our people be subjected to the cruel displacement's of an irrational economy - or is there a better way? Must we stand by while our liberties are undermined, our resources squandered, our environment polluted - or is there a better way? Must private profit be the nation's driving force - or is there a better way?" (The Progressive, 1976:5)

"The Big Divide" Kathrine Fong quotes in The Herald. "It's ironic that despite our ever increasing knowledge and more sophisticated tools to deal with the challenges, we still can' t close the divide. Many of us watch helplessly as it widens, feeling, perhaps, its inevitability: In an era of limits, growth and prosperity for some means less for others." "Even readers with advanced educations and seasoned careers experience difficulties." "Some have lost faith that government or the private sector can provide solutions, or that individual action will have any impact." "Some have lost confidence in humanity." "Many have lost heart." A worried Miami resident Elias Martin likens America's current problem to that in third world Latin America quoting, "When the middle class vanishes, there is a lot more tension between the other groups, which is what we are seeing now." It's time for us to wake up and smell the coffee! Is this our destiny? The choice is yours my friends!!!!

[Illustration 10]

Sociologists study social sciences through two countering view points. One being the Order perspective, usually adopted by the wealthy and powerful. Second is the Conflict perspective, usually adopted by the poor and powerless. Fortunately most sociologists tend to lean more toward the conflict perspective, since it more closely describes our American society. Due to my personal experiences, observations of my peer groups and the fact my wife and I were previously a comfortable middleclass family, I will lean heavily toward the conflict perspective.

ORDER MODEL

1) People in positions of power occupy bureaucratic roles necessary for the rational accomplishments of society's objectives.
2) The state works for the benefit of all. Laws reflect the customs of society and ensures order, stability, and justice – in short, the common good.
3) Pluralism: (a) competing interest groups; (b) majority rules; (c) power is diffused.

CONFLICT MODEL

1) People in positions of power are motivated by their own self interests.
2) The state exists for the benefit of the ruling class (law, police, courts protect the interests of the wealthy).
3) Power is concentrated in the power elite (the rich).

In American society, the societal stratifications have always existed. However, they had existed with a more fair distribution of wealth and power until the past decade. Basically, the rich to poor ratio wasn't so contrasting. In the past seven to ten years, we have witnessed American capitalism take an abhorrent turn for the worst and adopt a new greedier posture. Now we are seeing a form of socio-economic totalitarianism being forced on the working masses by the wealthy elite minority. This overclass is literally molding society's status quo to benefit them now more than before in previous years. Whether this is some orchestrated plan or plot on behalf of this overclass, or it's the so called "greed factor", totally out of control, leading to an anarchic law of the jungle, survival of the fittest, assault on society, we aren't sure.

America, always being a middleclass society where the majority lived relatively comfortable, is now undergoing a terrible transformation. Newsweek magazine May 1, 1995, Rich Thomas in his article "A Rising Tide Lifts The Yachts", quotes; "Yes the rich are getting richer, and the poor get poorer. At least that's what a study on wealth across the country - and the world - seems to show." He also adds; "In fact the United States leads the industrialized world in it's inequality of incomes. The haves, have more now than at any time, since 1929. Absolutely, and it's increasing. In 1969 the top 20% of American households received 7.5 times the income of the bottom fifth. By 1992, the richer households had 11 times the income of the poor. By contrast, the rich-to-poor ratio in Canada and Britain was about 7 to 1 in 1992; in Germany it was just 5.5 to one half the U.S. inequality rate."

This makes me remember the day I was talking to some German tourists on Miami beach. I had a brief conversation with them about the economy of America and my own demoralizing loss of the middleclass lifestyle. They couldn't see how Americans were surviving. I discussed a few wage levels of careers for both professional trades and careers requiring a

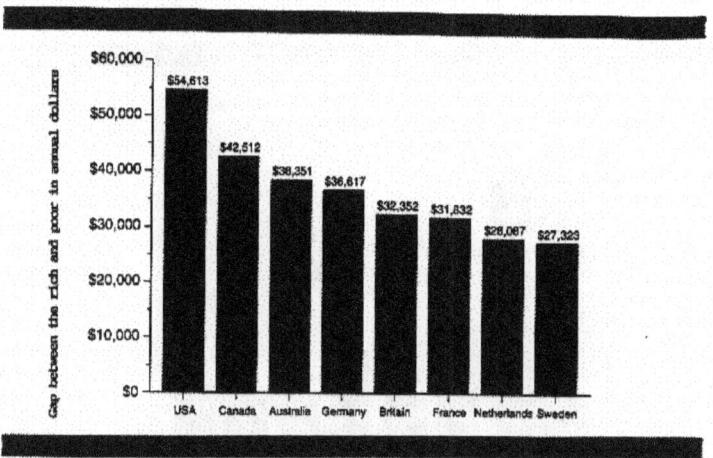

THE WIDEST GAP

Standing out in the crowd! Heads above the rest! The one time we do not wish to stand out in the crowd, we are caught reaching for the stars. The United States has the largest gap between the rich and the poor, than any other developed nation in the world. The American poor, at $10,923 per year, earn almost half of Sweden's poor who earn about $18,129 per year. I thought America had the highest standard of living in the world? Boy have we been fooled!!! The fall of Babylon. It appears the grass is greener on the other side of the fence now!

[Illustration 11]

27

THE HIGHEST POVERTY RATE

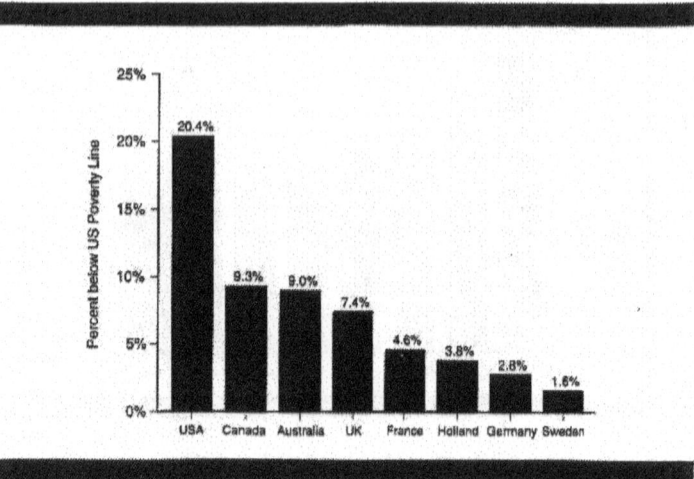

The black sheep of the family. The U.S. leads the flock, over the entire developed world, in the greatest number of children living in poverty. And it is increasing! What future is there for the children of tomorrow? It seems the future is only for the children of the rich. An exclusive club indeed!

[Illustration 12]

28

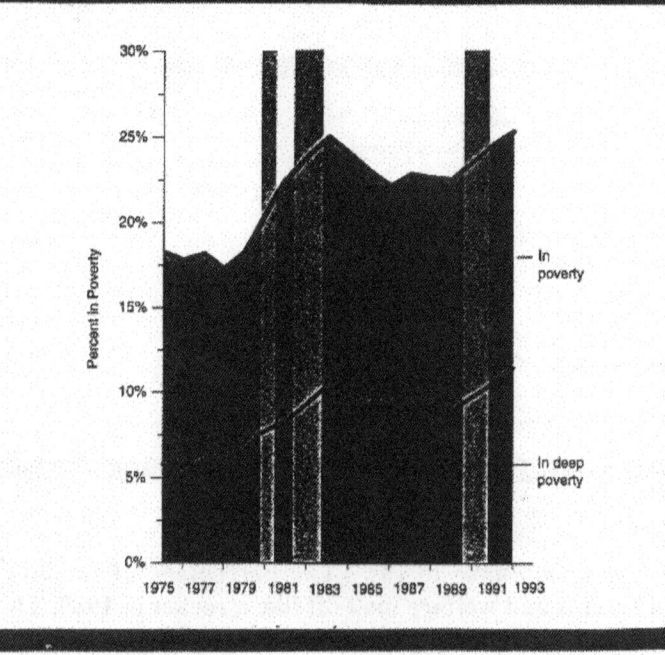

Just when you thought it could not get any worse think again! The poorest of the poor are suffering even more. How much farther down can they go?

[Illustration 13]

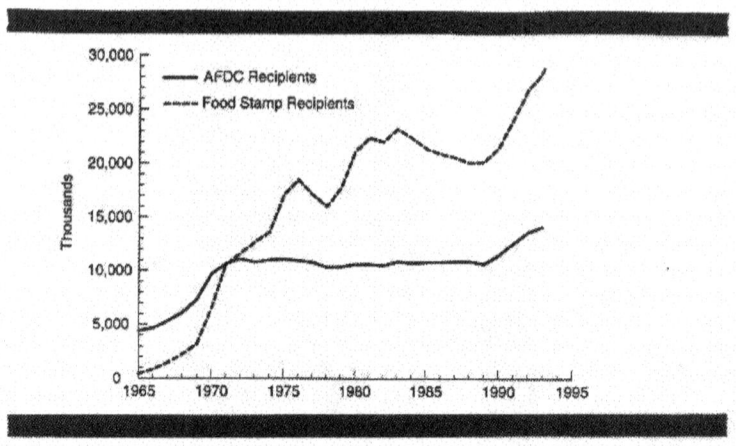

Even the poor have to eat. The percentage of families on food stamps and welfare took off like a rocket in 1989. This is about the same time American corporations started the largest re-organizational scale backs of all time, and working America's wages really started to decline.

[Illustration 14]

college degree. They commented asking "what happened to America?" and were stunned at how little we pay our workers. They also commented that our income to cost of living was intolerable, after I gave them some examples. Before they parted, they commented on the large number of homeless people in Miami. These tourists claimed to have been to other large European cities - Brussels, Paris, London and Rome. They didn't remember seeing so many homeless. They claimed people in Germany with trades training and college degrees would earn much more money than a comparable American citizen. Mind you, Germany is a free democratic society like America !!

Mr. Thomas also quoted in his article; "Europe achieves greater equality because of it's taxes and spends more for social programs, sets higher minimum wages and exercises more control over employment conditions and other benefits."

Realizing that Europe has finally surpassed the U.S. in standards of living for it's workers, this further strengthened my adamant support of more government regulation of corporate America. If Europe now has it better for the worker, then it is high time to dump corporate deregulation of the past several presidential terms and get America back on to it's feet. America used to have the highest standard of living. What does that tell you? **"Don't leave the fox in charge of the hen house!!!!"**

Have you ever heard of the old saying "money talks, bull_ _ _ t walks !!" Well that saying isn't going to get any truer than it is today! Let's get back to basics.

In the United states there are roughly 20,000 lawyers, public relations experts, association executives and technical workers known as lobbyists. The job of these lobbyists is to speak, and work for interest groups. They influence legislatures and regulatory agencies to pass legislation, laws and decisions most beneficial to their particular groups of interest. The lobbyists use a variety of ways of doing this. They entertain, give information, do favors, give campaign contributions to potential political representatives, furnish transportation, and send congress telegrams. In a sense, just legal bribery!

The facts show that most lobbyists are financed by the wealthy capitalist power elite, and therefore they only push for matters that directly or indirectly effect the wealthy. In other words, ensure the wealthy elite get their way most of the time. Ever heard of the phase, "do not bite the hand that feeds you?" Lobbyists? Well this is apparently the definition!

31

NOW PLAYING IN A SOCIETY NEAR YOU "DON'T BITE THE HAND THAT FEEDS YOU !"

Starring Sharky B. Greedy, co-starring Lobbyist B. Bribe and Uncle Sam.

[Illustration 15]

There are basically two viewed forms of power distribution in America. The elitist model, and the pluralist. The pluralist model, however has two viewpoints, the representative democracy and the veto groups. The elitist model has three viewpoints, power elite 1, power elite 2, and power elite 3. Adding these sub-titles, there are really five viewpoints of power distribution in America. Have you ever heard the saying, "If it looks like a duck, walks like a duck, swims like a duck and quacks like a duck, it must be a duck!"?

Now for a little sociology lesson to see what these five viewpoints have in common.

Oh well, here are the five ducks!

Pluralist viewpoint #1: Representative Democracy. In a democratic form of government, like the United States, the people supposedly have the power. The desires, will and the ideas of the majority prevail for the good of the majority. Since we are a very large society, we can not make all of the decisions, therefore, we elect representatives to speak for us. After electing these representatives, we expect them to follow through with their promises. Unfortunately in reality, we have been deceived many times, and are quite powerless. We all have learned through experience that both Democratic and Republican representatives are alike in two ways. They both can be corrupted and answer to a higher God, the almighty dollar.

How political campaigns are financed is the un-democratic feature of this viewpoint. Political campaigning is the most expensive task a candidate will ever undertake in his/her career. The campaign staff, mail advertisement, phone banks, computers, equipment, polling, consultants, media advertising, printing costs, television advertising and God knows what else, can run into the $ millions. Example: A presidential campaign can run roughly $1.5 billion.

The massive funding for this comes from the federal government (a major presidential candidate receives roughly $70 million in federal moneys), the rest is supplied by wealthy citizens, political parties, his own wealth, and political action committees or PACS.

A typical senate seat can run $4 million. A re-election running senator would have to raise $12,500 a week for about six years.

PACS, however are financed by special interest groups. Who do we suppose finances these special interest groups? You guessed it! Lobbyists! Somebody has to finance the lobbyists. Last but not least, our ravenous, money hungry shark, the wealthy power elite capitalists.

There are two other ways for wealthy individuals and special interest groups to sneak money to a candidate. Since each individual can only legally give up to $1,000, wealthy executives each pool his/her $1,000 donation into one pot. Then a nice sizable and juicy contribution (bribe) can be offered to the candidate of their choice.

The second legal way, is to donate what is called soft money to the candidate. This soft money is donated in unlimited quantities by rich individuals, wealthy corporations and other powerful organizations, to political parties at local, state and national levels. Then the political parties give directly to the candidates. In this method, which basically bypasses the laws, there are no limits to the amount of the contribution. Basically legalized bribery. This soft money loophole was ultimately abused, the first time, by the wealthy corporate elite and rich citizens, to grease the palms of both Republican and Democratic candidates in the 1988 and 1992 elections. As the Dallas Times quoted; "The power of PAC money threatens to turn members of congress into legalized political prostitutes. It drives them to sell to the highest bidders their one most easily and legally salable product – access. But worst of all, it erodes the public's confidence in the integrity of the congressional system." (quoted in Wertheimer, 1986:60)

Pluralist viewpoint #2 veto groups. Inevitably, certain groups are more dominant than others, and so are individuals. According to this viewpoint, a mass number of interest groups are concerned only with their own interests. The outcome is a neutralization of power. The masses are supposedly supported in their exertion of power on issues that effect them. Under ideal conditions, these groups aren't supposed to pay any attention to the power deviations from the various interest groups. In reality only a fool would believe that the mass relentless power and tremendous financial resources of the wealthy capitalists and their families could be curbed by the meager resources of the middleclass, poor or a handful of united farmers. The downfall here is that the leaders of the various groups come primarily from the wealthy overclass. The possibility of an ominous coalition elite, that overshoots the ideas of the narrow interest groups that aren't appropriately financed, does likely exist. Again, law of the jungle, survival of the fittest.

Do you know of the saying "birds of the same feather, flock together."? Well there you go!

The second viewpoint is the Elitest models. Karl Marx, the father of modern day communism, believed that the capitalistic stratification of society meant unequal distribution of resources, money, rewards and ultimately power. The wealthy elite (overclass) exerts an tremendous, unfair manipulation of the federal government's policies and actions through it's financial domination of the nation' s economy. Marx also believed that citizens (masses) were molded and manipulated by the elite through patriotism, nationalism, religion, media and press control, control of high profile governmental leaders and propaganda. Ultimately, the government is a mighty tool of the wealthy ruling class to get their way.

This sounds horribly true of the predicament we are facing in America today. That is too scary, that a Communist leader could accurately predict the demise of the middleclass and the poor in America. This sends chills up and down my spine! This further supports the urgency and need far every man and woman in America to stop this greedy "in your face capitalism" abomination, before civil unrest occurs. History has proven, time and time again, that a desperate, financially oppressed people could inadvertently elect a Communist style party into power to prevent any further slide in the standard of living. Anti-democratic movements know this. **It is imperative that this problem be stopped now, to guarantee the preservation of ethical capitalism, democracy and freedom in America !!!! We must not let the predictions of a communist leader come**

true! The enemy political powers of the world are watching us now more than before. What price are we willing to pay for insatiable corporate greed?

Power Elite # 1, The thesis of C. Wright Mills. Mills believed that there are three sectors of power, the wealthy corporate rich, the executive branch, and the military branch of the government. The top executives of each sector combine to form a power elite. They make all the important decisions of the country. The sectors are dependent on each other. These form three levels in Mill's power pyramid. The top part of the pyramid consists of executive leaders from the three sectors. Forming the point of the pyramid, the most powerful of the three sectors is the corporate elite rich. The second in power is the executive branch of the government. The last in power is the military branch. The second level, forming the middle of the pyramid consists of the interest groups, legislative branches and opinion leaders. The third level, forming the base of the pyramid consists of the unorganized, ignorant masses. These brow beaten and unconcerned masses can easily be coerced, manipulated and controlled from above. They are there to be used, exploited politically, economically and socially for the benefit of the wealthy power elite. If there is any kind of mass plot or conspiracy on behalf of this rich corporate overclass, this would be the most logical way they would exercise power. Kind of makes you feel like a usable commodity, a field full of crops or a barn yard full of animals, doesn't it? Once again we must halt this abomination of the overclass. **Our founding fathers did not intend for it to be this way!!** The obvious reason the masses got into this situation in the first place is their unconcerned, footloose attitudes, total ignorance or they are too busy with daily life to give a rat's a_ _! Maybe a combination of these factors. Or just possibly, the people could be much more concerned with the status of their favorite movie stars, which soap opera to watch or with their favorite sporting events, Super Bowl, World Series or the Stanley Cup Playoffs.

"The social pacifier," Sports to the big silver screen are our priorities nowadays. Imagine, for one moment if the Super Bowl, World Series, or a TV series starring some of societies most admired super stars was permanently canceled. There would be protests with unity of the likes never seen before, mass demonstrations, picket lines around Federal buildings, civil disobedience on the verge of civil war. However, witness mass employee violations, lay several hundred thousand workers off, give 30 million people a dollar an hour pay cut, and you probably won't hear so much as a peep. The house is burning down, and we are standing with the hose in our hands worrying about the tulips under our windows. Snap out of it America!!! If half the people who watched the Super Bowl protested the erosion of the middle class standard of living, we wouldn't be in the fix we are in today. You are making the bed, now you are going to have to sleep in it!! The choice is yours!

[Illustration 16]

Power elite #2, Domhoff's "Governing Class Theory". Domhoff defines this governing class as the rich upper class or over-class, approximately 5% of the American population. This over-class consists of the wealthy capitalists and their families, which controls an unfair, disproportionate amount of the country's wealth. They also appoint a disproportionate amount of leaders to the country's decision and controlling organizations. Domhoff believes this ruling class controls the executive and judicial branches of the federal government. Thus congress is efficiently and effectively blocked on two of three fronts. Therefore, all American domestic and foreign policies are proposed, passed and enforced by organizations loyal to the power elite. The final result, all policies passed benefit mainly the rich. Domhoff also believes the upper-class power elite get their way by force or fraud. The masses will not liberate themselves from this situation because of their lack of concern or the status quo (that's the way things go and there is nothing anybody can do!) factor. The people are broken and timid to the point of passiveness. They are told lies to the point of satisfaction by those in power even though the results are not evident. In other words fooled into accepting the actions of the decision makers were made in their best interests even though they really were not.

Power Elite #3, Parenti's "Bias of The System Theory". In America the power is concentrated among the wealthy, whom control all facets of the government and the largest most powerful corporations. These few thousand wealthy individuals came from overly wealthy backgrounds, filled with power and prestige. These demi-gods and their mighty corporations set the trends of the economy, dictating production, consumption, resource development and use, employment, unemployment, prices of goods, workers wage standards, foreign trade, and ultimately our standard of living and lifestyle. The people (masses) and small businesses are at their mercy. There was a time, not too long ago, when the heads of small business made all the decisions affecting the economy. Now, only the most powerful corporations virtually control the entire economy.

Parenti viewed this super corporate elite as having virtually molded society, the masses and status quo to their benefit utilizing their juggernaut powers. This is accomplished by brute force, psychological and social conditioning, propaganda and brain washing over a period of time. This supreme over-class controls the definition of financial, family, social values and ultimately life itself in America. This can also be accomplished through education, family and society values and religion. Example: How many times have you been told by parents, teachers, society in general, to work hard and do whatever (suck up) to please your boss, and you'll be very successful earning lots of money. Unfortunately, today most hard work goes un-noticed, not getting the rewards it deserves, unless you are very lucky or in the right place at the right time.

Parenti claims that by using these tools, we are taught that the current system is the only way, and our roles in society are to be accepted as the norm (status quo). In this socialization process, the masses are conditioned (brainwashed) to accept the system's ideas and obey all laws, regulations and decisions no matter how detrimental they are to them. Like a battered wife or an abused child, the masses accept layoffs, pay/benefit cuts, increases in costs of living, declines in quality of life and standards of living with out so much as a fuss. Continuing all of these techniques, the power elite get their way without so much as lifting a finger to silence the masses. The battle is over before it is ever stared!

Today in America, it is clearly obvious that, one or a combination of these forms of power distribution, coupled with the "greed factor", are at play. We all have had our share of layoffs, pay/benefit cuts and decay in the standard of living. Yet the wealthy corporate over-class continues to reap record profits and personal income gains. The million dollar question is: How long are we going to let this escalating problem go before doing something??

"THE SLOW SQUEEZE" Corporate America is using social conditioning by gradually raising employment requirements, slowly cutting pay scales and benefits, freezing salaries or lowering them each time a new employee is hired. By doing this over many years, the income standards of working America and the American standards of living are being inconspicuously lowered. Ironically, these same corporations gradually raise the costs of their goods and services to the masses and small businesses. Like some ghastly parasite, they are sucking at both ends, becoming gorged with higher profits and pay for the CEOs and upper management.

[Illustration 17]

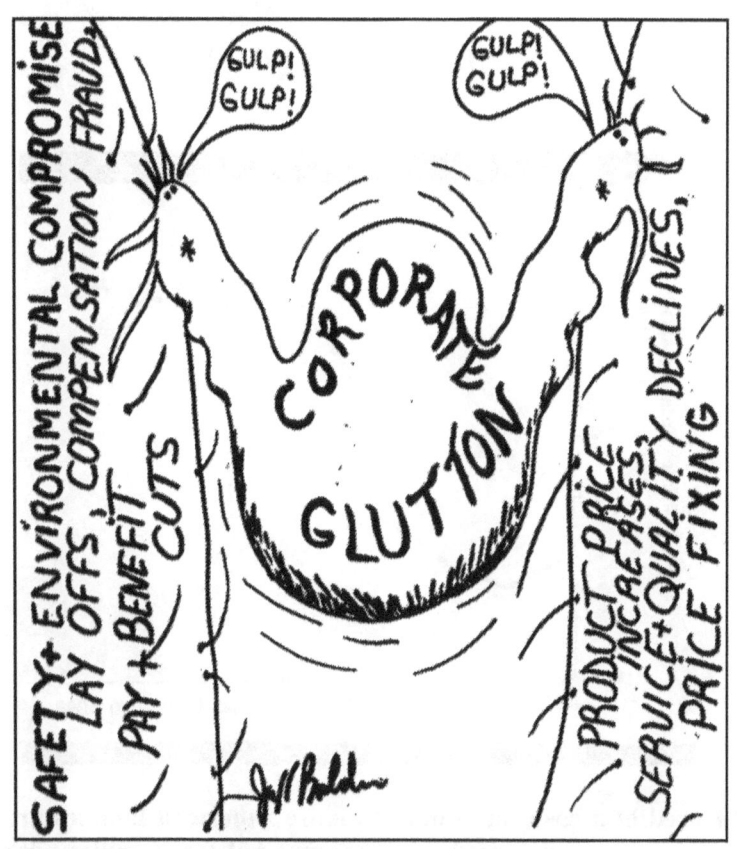

"It double sucks!!!!" The ghastly parasite! It is time to loose the leaches, supporting only those corporations willing to invest in people, and the future of vibrant America, instead of investing in the upper management's and Ceo's wallets!!!

[Illustration 18]

FAMIILIES RECEIVING AID

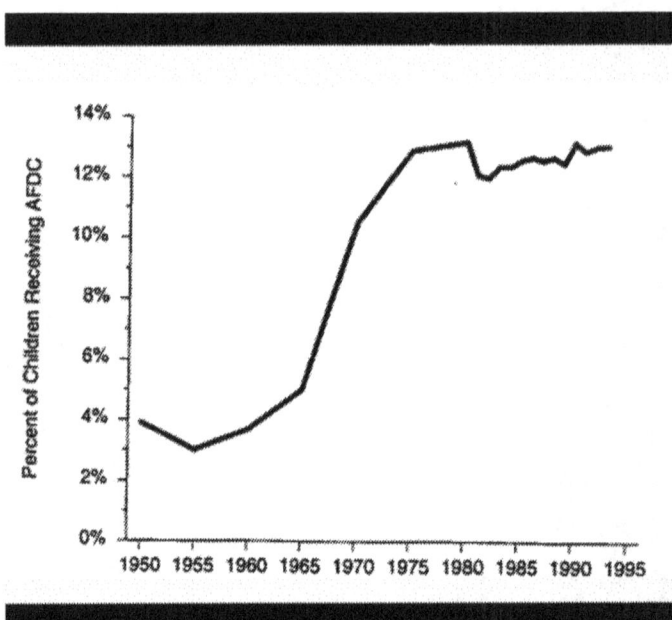

In need of a cash hand out. As more American families are earning less and forced into poverty, Aid for Families with Dependent Children (A.F.D.C.) is shelling out more benefits at record levels.

[Illustration 19]

DECLINING MONTHLY WELFARE PAYMENTS

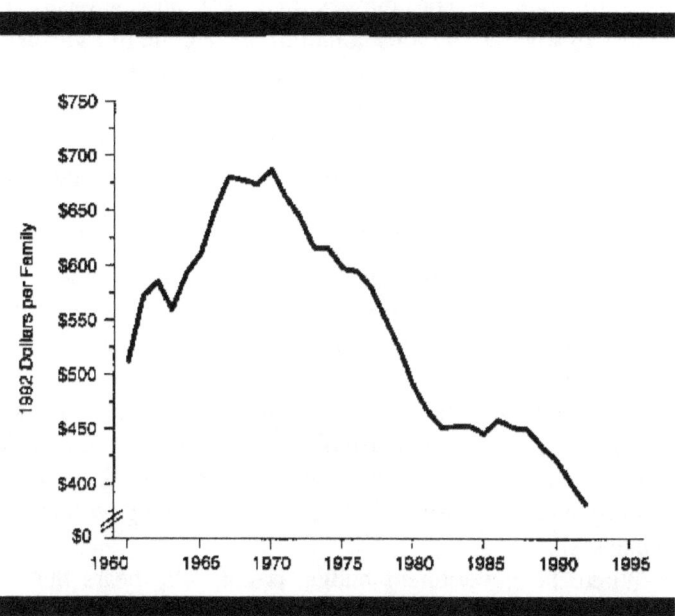

Just to rub salt into the wounds. As more American families needed these survival hand outs, the amount paid out was reduced to half of the 1970,s rate. Do you think the cost of living in the 1990,s went down to the levels of the 1950,s????

[Illustration 20]

No matter how we cut these five ducks, they all taste the same with the rich getting richer, the middleclass and poor getting poorer. Small business, middleclass and poor families will foot the bill and suffer the consequences.

When our economy is up, who usually benefits? The wealthy corporate leaders! The masses may get an increase in the quantity of low paying jobs, a halt in the decline of their pay and benefits and if they are lucky, an insignificant raise in pay. Either way, not really enough to offset inflation.

When the economy is down, who benefits? The rich over-class! The masses endure massive layoffs, heavy pay/benefit cuts, overburdening work quotas and responsibilities and ultimately a lower standard of living. However, the wealthy CEOs, and upper management maintain their incomes or still receive decent pay increases. It's ironic that the masses are used like a giant fat reserve to enable the corporate leaders to survive the bad times.

When the interests of the over-class clash with the needs and desires of the masses, who usually gets their way? The wealthy!

During a national dilemma, who bears the bulk of the costs and burdens of the responsibilities? Usually the government and the masses!

When the government budget is cut, who bears the cross? Usually the poor and the middleclass (powerless masses). Declines in social programs, student assistance programs, state health programs for the financially burdened, and cut backs on government policing programs to ensure corporate adherence to rules and regulations.

When the government enacts a military draft, who is least likely to be drafted? During the Vietnam war, only 10% of all college students were drafted. If a college student is drafted, his chances of serving an the front lines is much less than a non-college poor man.

When the government passes out tax cuts, who usually gets the lion's share? The wealthy elite through generous tax incentives, new tax shelters and huge write-off privileges.

The most alarming evaluation was done by Robert Hutchins in his critique of government policy relating to domestic affairs.

He quoted; "Domestic policy is conducted according to one infallible rule: the costs and burdens of whatever is done must be born by those least able to bear them". (Hutchins, 1976:4) In other words, the delight of the overclass at the expense of everyone else!

If this un-thinkable, grotesque policy is being practiced on Capital Hill, then the responsibility of the American people is more urgent than ever to take a united stance against this socio-econimic rape and exploitation!!!! We cannot assume, under any circumstances, that our government will do what is beneficial for the majority. For all we know, corruption could be running rampant on Capital Hill. We have to voice our disapproval of this demoralizing policy and prove we will not stand for it!! Our founding fathers intended for the people to have the right and power to change anything inhumane or demoralizing in our government. They gave us this right!!!! Only the people, nobody else, can return the country to the original plan laid out by the founding fathers. I think it is about time to start exercising these rights!!!

I want to stress one thing. The American system is the best system on the planet, at least in theory, and gave most people the American dream not too long ago. It worked once, it can be repaired and will work again.

Even unemployment is beneficial to the corporate overclass. Here are a few examples:

1) Unemployed and poor people are willing to perform back breaking labor and will work long inhumane hours for meager wages with little or no benefits.

2) The military drafts are avoided by the children of the rich, because of the willingness of the poor, or unemployed to join voluntarily just trying to survive.

3) Labor unions yield much less power during periods of high unemployment, and employees are less likely to organize.

4) Workers are more likely to tolerate hazardous conditions and perform dangerous tasks. They are less likely to demand expensive safety equipment and time consuming safety procedures.

5) The wealthy corporate leaders and their families, do not have to pay their fare share of taxes. The government gives them massive tax incentives, hoping to encourage them to expand creating new jobs.

6) The most terrible of all, to fester and maintain social, racial, sexual and economic bias amongst the working class masses. They estimate, that the more energy exhausted quarreling over these matters, creates a lovely diverting smoke screen to the ultimate goal of the overclass. The goal here is to prevent any possibilities of massive organization, much less any cooperation between racial, gender and economic lines. Thus, all threats are stamped out before they became a problem.

All the research done by the experts, and what we've learned up to now, indicates this trend is going to continue and the situation will get worse. With the "greed factor" as the life blood of this terrible beast, power and resources will continue to be directed away from the masses and more toward the wealthy overclass. Resulting in greed factor that is totally out of control!!!!

We could, very well, be witnessing the largest and most unthinkable plot in history, launched against a society, a people and a lifestyle.

This elite could be attempting to break the cohesion and spirit of the middleclass and underclass. Thus guaranteeing more wealth, power and profits in the future with the least amount of resistance. We are a barely tapped natural resource ripe for the picking. The reaper is sharpening his blade! Guess what? It's harvest time!!!!!!!!

Chapter 4 The effects of downward mobility. The rape of a lifestyle

They say it is more painful to have once had, than it is to have never had! This couldn't be any truer. This has happened not only to me and most members our entire family, but to a good percentage of friends and co-workers.

I am the son of a proud small business man. I saw my father start small, and realized his devotion to his fledgling business in Maryland was un-fathomable. They were like his children, that he nurtured patiently. On many instances he was called a workaholic by all the members of our family. He saw the American Dream and pursued it, even sacrificing home and family to the cause. My sister, brother and I eventually accepted not having him home to play with us. We realized he was on a quest, that he was determined to undertake. It was what he wanted to do!

I remember the day, and joy on his face, when he opened a small airport shuttle bus service in Atlanta, Georgia. As his business grew and branched out, he was like a child with a new toy. He created his little empire in the transportation, time share and travel business. This was his perfect little world to dream and ponder in. However, there was a storm on the horizon.

By the late 1980's the economic forecast was calling for a category 4 hurricane. The great depression of 1990-91, as I call it, hit. My father is a proud man and shows little emotion, especially when it comes to grieving. As his little world began to crumble in the ferocious winds, his armor got a crack in it, and he began to take on water. I only know from a reliable source, that the "man of steel" was reduced to a whimpering, shaking child.

His world came down hard on all of us. His corporation being in a non-essential service related business, geared to pleasure, turned out to be it's weakness in the new economic environment. With mass layoffs, pay cuts, plunges in the family incomes and drops in the standard of living becoming status quo, people put the squeeze on their wallets. The extra funds reserved for vacations and pleasures, became survival funds far most people, and the demand for vacation travel, pleasure spending declined considerably.

At about this time, my family and I began feeling the fringes of this great storm. I had been working as a technician, selling services and servicing customers, for a large regional pest control firm in Pompano Beach Florida. I worked hard and was excellent at my work, after being with them for almost 8 years. In 1988, I had earned technician of the month, and in 1989, I had earned technician of the year. Most of all, I was rewarded handsomely for my expertise!

I was newly married at the time, and my annual income was roughly $28,000. Not too shabby at all for a blue collar income household! We lived a couple of blocks from the beach, in a comfortable apartment in Pompano Beach. The rent for this beautiful place was $400 a ninth. Gosh!, we earned that in about 3 days! We had one new car at the time and the payments were about $200 and some change. Another couple of days income to cover these major family expenses. To be conservative, in a week and a half, we covered the largest expenses in the middleclass lifestyle. That left us with another two and a half weeks of income to cover food, utilities, clothing, recreation and savings. We even started to save for a house of our own. After thinking job security was here to stay. I felt confident to buy a 19 foot cuddy cabin power boat to nurture my growing interests in scuba diving and underwater photography. I had excellent credit with all of the major credit card companies, and department stores. The credit card bills were under control, with some having no balance at all.

We could go out on Friday nights to eat at the local bistros, Bennigan's, T.G.I. Friday's Etc. A trip to the grocery store was a pleasurable delight, since about $70 bought about six bags of groceries, enough to last a week and a half. A visit to the movies was a popular event for us. I used to go to the local firing range, to fire off a box of 9mm rounds. I loved to practice marksmanship at the gun ranges, with my Glock pistol. A gallon of gasoline was between 79¢ to 83¢. You can bet the boat was out most every weekend for a cruise, a round of fishing or scuba diving. We were even able to help some of the older members of the family. Most of our family, friends and co-workers were living similar lifestyles. The American Dream was sweet indeed!

In late 1990, the first band of squalls, of this storm hit and the forcast of an economic depression seemed more likely. The company I was working for changed it's pay plan from an hourly pay scale to a commission percentage scale per job completed. Without the hourly pay plus the legal number of overtime hours, I lost close to $200 a week in income. The quotas and performance expectations were also increased, requiring more time and responsibilities on my part. The new company goal was to spend much less time in the customer's home and shift from quality of work to quantity. As service men we were pressured to stop taking the time to do it right, but to complete as many homes in a day as possible. Yet the prices of the services to the clients started to climb radically for less quality work. Customer complaints went through the roof, and the technician got the blame for not doing the job properly. The working stress was mounting and the pay checks were shrinking! This was my first taste of "in your face capitalism".

To rub salt into the wound, our rent went up $100 a month and food prices started to climb. Well, we were forced to move inland away from the beach to escape rent increases. That too was soon in vain. A few months after the move, that rent jumped $50 a month and started a gradual $25 a month increase every few months.

After several months of feeling the strangle-hold, I figured a career change would be in my best interest. The career as a tractor trailer driver seemed to fit the bill. I had a few friends driving the eighteen wheelers around, making at least $14 an hour. Hey that was $3 an hour more than I was making on the hourly program at the pest control firm. I could settle for that!!!! After all, I could pay for the big rig course with my spotless credit.

The first day at the school proved that I wasn't the only one with a career change in mind! The instructors were shocked by the 300% increase in enrollment in the last several months. The school was so they had to rent portable class rooms and 4 extra semi trucks. By the time I was ready to graduate from the seven week course, there was a six month waiting list for new students. It appeared that after conversing with my class mates from all different career back grounds, the declining income story was the same for these young men and women.

Graduation finally came and I was ready to stop living off of savings and start hauling in the big bucks with big trucks. I was in for a rude awakening, when I hit the job market. After several interviews, I learned I was in the second mass wave of new tractor trailer graduates looking for work requiring a class A CDL drivers license. This spelled serious trouble, now there were more people on the job market than there were jobs! Soon after graduation one of my friends lost his $14 an hour truck driving job to a driver, fresh out of school, earning only $10 an hour. That wasn't the end of it! This started a terrible domino effect, and whom ever would work for less would get the job and so on! and so on!

By late 1991, about two months into my new career, I realized I was not going to find any jobs paying more than $9 an hour. I also noticed tremendous increasing turnover amongst workers in general. It seemed like every day there was a new face replacing somebody else. I started to notice a trend, that people were being replaced just before there probationary period was up and their benefits were due to kick in. Well, one week before my benefits were due to kick in, I ended up being next. The reason for termination was a small altercation with a loading dock causing only minor damage almost two months before. These type of things happened to just about everyone at one time or another. Nobody is perfect we are all human. I found out from some inside sources that just about everyone was being fired for supposedly little mistakes. It the company would keep track of even the most trivial error, not just driving errors, on the employee's part to later use against them as a reason for termination. Even more senior employees found themselves on the un-employment line, being replaced by workers working for $3 to $5 less an hour.

Well, time went by and I had at least seven more similar experiences. I, however, noticed that these companies would run job position adds in the classified sections every week of the year for the same positions. Since there seemed to be no shortage of applicants, it looked as though they were running an employment assemble line. Just keep rolling in the front door and shoving them out the back door, NEXT!!!

After a three year period of time, averaging 4 jobs a year, I was down to $7 an hour to operate these giant semi trucks. I now realized there was something fishy here!! I wasn't going to operate these eighteen wheelers, much less shift the gears, for a dollar or two more than a kid flipping burgers in a fast food joint. Good God man!!!! I made those wages back in 1982 driving a small 26 foot furniture van! My last job offer paid a meager $6.50 an hour to operate a tractor and trailer combination of about 60+ feet in length. I looked the boss in the face and chuckled. I asked him "how am I supposed to support my family on those wages!!" I commented, I earned that over ten years ago. He replied with an attitude, "That's not my problem! Besides, why should I pay you any more when drivers are a dime a dozen these days" He then commented that he was looking for a single man, or a retired person with no family or large financial obligations to pay almost minimum wages. He then stated he would have never hired a family man because they wouldn't stay with him and he wanted to keep turnover down. Well, since he was up front, respecting me wishing me the best of luck, I shook his hand and returned the favor and the good luck part. He will need it too! It was absolutely un-believable, since most employers were apparently searching for these ideal persons with no financial responsibilities to pay as little as possible. It was clearly apparent, I stumbled on what was causing that fishy smell! Our greedy, money hungry, capitalist shark!!!!

Well, I finally found what looked like a steady job for more than a 90 day period of time. I had started to work driving a giant semi-truck flatbed combination with a pre-fab concrete structure company. My duty was to transport these massive concrete structures, sometimes weighing over 100 tones, with permits, escorts, flashing lights and flags, all over the state of Florida. Not an easy job, especially when starting pay was $8 an hour. After almost a year there, I noticed the company had something against repairing the trucks and especially the trailers when something broke. As drivers we would constantly hound them about unsafe equipment, but we were always ordered to operate the vehicle anyway! They always put it off sometimes for several months, or when an incident occurred. Then ironically if something did happen the driver would then get blamed, written up or fired. Well, I had my share of write-ups, only a total of three per employee, before termination. I was finally fired after a concrete structure crumbled due to vibration of the road, sending rocks raining on to the cars following me. This was something totally out of my control, but the supervisor said this was my third write up, and he would have to let me go! It appeared we were the fall guys for their negligence. I new this was true, since I befriended one of the dispatchers, whom would occasionally take a load himself when drivers were short. He had gotten fired shortly after I was. This was after he and several other employees, my self included, had repeatedly told management of cracked suspension springs on one of the trailers. He had warned them a serious accident was waiting to happen. One day he ended up with a load on that trailer bound for Naples Florida. After arriving in Naples, he was exiting the expressway ramp suddenly, he heard a loud crack and the whole trailer, with a heavy load, listed to one side, eventually turning over pulling the tractor over with it. Luckily, he only was going 25 mph and only suffered minor injuries, and no other motor vehicles were involved. The company terminated his employment for operating company equipment un-safely. Yeah right!! He took the heat for someone else's greed and incompetence!

My wife started to have her taste of "In your face capitalism" too! Little as she knew it, the fin was in the water and circling in for the kill. After a complicated pregnancy, our first baby, a little girl, was born a couple of months premature. Her esophagus was under developed and with a possibility of kidney dialysis. This required regular visits to Miami Children's Hospital, as well as, her pediatrics for tests and monitoring development. My wife's supervisors had reluctantly given her the time, off to take the child to the doctors, as long as she made up the time. My wife more than made up the time! Sometimes putting in more hours than some of the other help. One day, she looked my wife in the face and asked her if anybody else could take the baby to the doctors. My wife replied No! She said her husband was on the road and her mother didn't drive. The supervisor quoted, "I will do what I have to do!!!" My wife replied, "do what you want to do, if my child is sick and has to go to the doctor, I am going to take her to the doctor. My wife reminded the supervisor a week before the next scheduled visit, to Miami Children's Hospital for some tests. Well, the supervisor had a change of heart. The supervisor told my wife, "Mrs. Baldwin I know your family is your first priority!, and my department, as well as the company could no longer tolerate this." She then, told my wife "that she already knew the decision she made between family and career!"

Well, my wife was terminated!!! The termination was due to continually tardy and missing too much work. When she was authorize by her supervisor, to came in late and take care of her chronic child. The capitalist shark had sunken it's teeth in, and lied all the while!

My wife was obviously a victim of status quo, honestly believing there was nothing she or anybody else could do! She said that's just life. Well, I wasn't going to let her give up that easily with out a good fight. After some serious coaxing and a long talk with the Department of Labor, we found out not only a state but a Federal law was violated. This law is the Family Leave Act. It basically protects employees from being terminated or replaced if they have to take time off from work to tend to a death, sick spouse, child, parent, or other family emergency. After consulting the Florida Bar association we had a list of attorneys to call. Little to our knowledge we would be in for the fight of our lives. Much to our surprise, non of the attorneys would handle the case. They explained that Florida is a right to work state. At first we didn't realize what they meant by this! They explained that in a right to

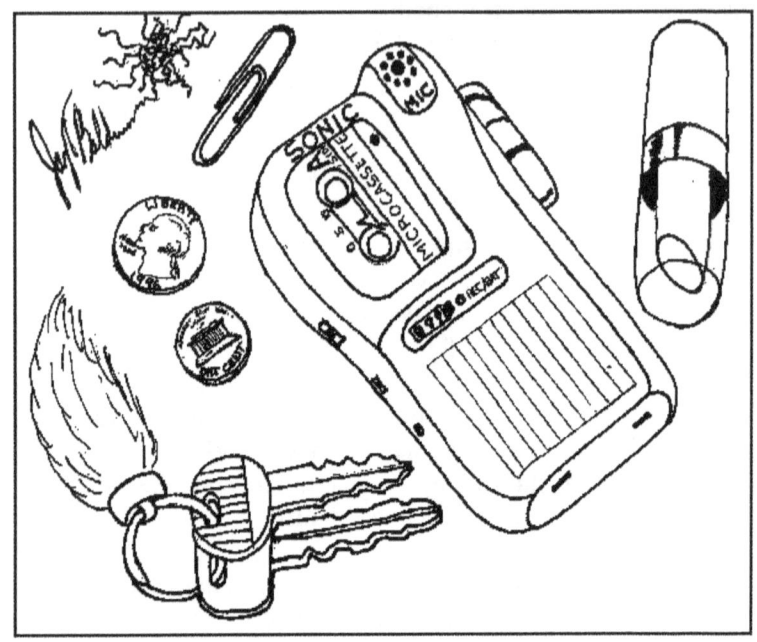

Sigh! You are on candid cassette!!! It's your word against theirs! So hold them to theirs forever! One of these placed inconspicuously in a front jacket, Front pants pocket, or in a cluttered purse is your most powerful, tactical weapon in obtaining hard sound evidence. Sad but true these days, the system, as well as society doesn't believe the average citizen over a high profile corrupted Dept., political leader, a spiteful supervisor or a corporation. In a court of law that could not be any truer. This little microcassette presented as evidence is a bombshell in turning any court in your favor almost every time! Available at an office supply store for $24-$40. Fight for your rights !! Use it!!

[Illustration 21]

work state, federal and state and local labor laws have no teeth in them, and an employer could virtually fire you for any reason under the sun. I was going to be damned if this company was going to get away with this !!! We finally convinced the branch of the Dept. of Labor known as the Equal Employment Opportunity Commission (E.E.O.C.) to handle the lawsuit case. Hey! we didn't even have to pay a penny for these attorneys, since it was a violation of written laws. <u>Absolutely</u> <u>free!!!!</u> However, they seemed to be convinced we would not stand a chance against this corporation. In our lawsuit we are requesting $60,000 in damages. After all we lost a car and were forced to move and go bankrupt, since my wife's position at this flower distribution Co. paid more than I was getting as a truck driver. After more than a year of haggling with this Dept. they ruled in favor of the corporation, and were going to drop the case! The reason for this was on grounds of not enough evidence. I was not sure if this was because of the right to work laws in Florida or corporate bribery! This really ticked me off!!!! We had at least three eyewitnesses to subpoena, paperwork and doctors. What more evidence did they need??? I was so sorry we didn't have a video camera handy when they fired my wife so we could get it on film! Well, I started to think. Then it hit me! Well I will just go over their heads. I started writing in depth protest letters to local mayors, the Governor of Florida, to the Florida senator in Washington D.C., all the way up to the President of the United States and his wife. Suddenly the wheels of justice started to turn! We received a reply directly from the President indicating names of people to contact, and re-assurances that the case will be re-evaluated and re-opened. Suddenly, everybody, everywhere was now more eager to work with us. Hey!, just put some Presidential heat under their feet and see how quick they dance for us. The case is now being taken very seriously, and even resulted in another letter from the White House indicating due to our case and similar cases, they were going to add some new amendments to the family leave laws.

We are on our fourth year of fighting the case. It seems persistence will pay off!! Our case is scheduled for late 1997.

Hey!, it ain't over to the fat lady sings!!!   No offense to my larger readers !!!

**CLUB I.R.S. A millionaire's exclusive experience.
Corporate ceo, Upper management, Overclass ID required.**

[Illustration 22]

By 1994 our joint tax return earnings were in the neighborhood of $19,000 with me working full time as a truck driver and my wife's part time job. Well, the boat had to go. I had to stop building model airplanes and the trips to the gun range had to quit.

The Family Leave Dilemma, a loosing proposition. " Fear of retaliation, coupled with the exhaustion brought an by family stress, keeps many workers from asserting their rights, says Ellen Bravo of 9 to 5, National Association of Working Women, an advocacy group." " The fear of retaliation looms large among employees who take time off for family, and the risk is rising. Though federal laws forbid retaliation against people who exercise their rights, employers can make leave-takers lives difficult in many ways." Quoted by Sue Shellenbarger, Work and Family Wall Street Journal. "Employees are more at risk than they've ever been," says Dee Soder of CEO Perspective Group, a New York executive-advisory concern. <u>Good</u> <u>God</u> <u>America</u> <u>Wake</u> <u>up!!</u> It is obvious that big business has no bounds of civilized decency or mercy, and is on the assault of the strongest pillar of American society, the American family unit. After articles like this, capital Hill should be flooded with letters of protest and protest marchers. America, what is it going to take to make you fight for human ethics and your rights ????

[Illustration 23]

By early 1994, all of our savings had dried up and we were well on our way to poverty. Almost as if to rub salt into the wound, we were forced to move two more times in a vain effort to avoid skyrocketing rents. Now our old apartment in Pompano was well over $900 a month. We finally, ended up in Miami, where the cheapest two bedroom, one bath I could find was $675 a month. This was just about three weeks take home salary on today's meager incomes! The neighborhood was far inland and nowhere as nice. I will be damned if we were going to live in a ghetto!!!!

Amidst all the bad news, I was un-expectedly offered another position back into the pest control field as a rout manager/sales inspector. This was with the nation's largest, "supposedly" most reputable and known termite and pest control company. I jumped on it, ready to put on the Robo-cop gig and start zapping bugs again. After all the truck driving career turned into a disaster and was not panning out. At first, the position appeared to my ticket out of poverty with a weekly gross salary roughly at $500. Performing services our hours were 50+ a week. I was on a commission based salary with an hourly compensation of about $11 an hour after 40 total weekly hours. I would also get a $50 bonus for every cross marketing lead that I turned in resulting in a sale, plus a standard sales commission for regular sales as well as the normal commission for servicing the new account. On top of it all we were allowed to take the company vehicle home with us. This meant I didn't need a car! This was excellent and the people I was working with had been there for many years. Turn over was very low! The job was a breeze since I had almost eight years experience in the field. After about six months the company started a re-organization campaign. A sweet term for layoffs. In short this meant layoffs for a lot of people. We lost most of the office staff. This meant most of the office work was to be handled by the rout managers/service technicians. Fortunately, to get the employees to accept the new plan, the extra hours and extra responsibilities, we were compensated hourly which doubled our overtime. We were now doing four jobs instead of one. We were now the service man, the appointment setter, the secretary and collection agent rolled up into one. We were expected to come home after a ten hour day on the field and put in another two to four hours at home making scheduling, appointment and answering customer complaint calls on top of collection calls and completing paperwork bringing all books up to date. Try to contact 20 plus families every night to set up schedules for the following day. This was no easy task as each time you called all the people on your list you would only contact one or two. Then you would have to wait 15 to 30 minutes and try again until you got them all. Basically we were slaves to the phone until we went to sleep. We could not leave the house at all, and this was the same on Saturdays and Sundays as we tried to get Monday's clients scheduled and to get caught up on all of the collection calls and paperwork not completed from the following week. They created two three ring binders we carried home every night with step by step procedures for all of this extra responsibility. A typical five day work week turned into a seven day a week, fourteen hour a day nightmare. We literally worked, slept and ate a meal, if we had time! Boy did the overtime go up with the size of our pay checks. All of this was a new company wide campaign to reach the billion dollar corporation by the year 2000. The slogan Vision 2000 posters, with all forms of propaganda phrases similar to a Hitler Third Reich fashion were hung all over the offices across the nation to unite all to one cause. Unfortunately, they started to pay the price as burnouts and employee turn over drastically increased.

It was barely a month into the new reich before a couple of corporate big shots came in from the corporate headquarters in Atlanta Georgia for a company wide meeting. The first thing addressed was the overtime situation. They claimed the overtime was way out of control and was sinking the company's budget. They then gave a long drawn out, propaganda loaded pep talk in an evangelist preaching style, that seemed to last hours. Oh!, how they talked, that we were one big family and with out the employees contributions across the board, the company will never reach vision 2000. They boasted how the stocks were expected to go ballistic and the profits were going to exceed that! This became almost a religious adventure to unite people to strive for this magical goal. Mind you!, all of this was going on over a catered pizza dinner compliments of the corporate headquarters. Then after, what seemed like an eternity, they dropped the bombshell. "We will no longer be able to compensate employees for all the extra overtime put in at home and on the weekends!" "Consider it your contribution to the vision 2000 cause!" "We know it will be very difficult on everybody not to get compensated for all the sacrificed time and effort, but think of all of the pride we will feel for our contributions!" You could almost hear the jaws of every one in that room hit the floor! Following a brief silence and bewildering looks on all faces, there started a grumbling roar that eventually had to be silenced by one of the branch managers. This meant we went from earning over $600 gross to just about $350 gross per week. Now if that wasn't a pay cut, then I don't know what one is!!!!!!!!!

One week went by and another big shot came down to have another company meeting to discuss the new medical insurance package. Yes! Another rate increase! Then he pulls out an envelope and reads it in front of all of us. He said that the use of company vehicles for all sales personnel was going to be terminated and sales personnel will be expected to use their personal vehicles on company business. They would paid $30 a week to start for gas. He also added that service technicians will no longer take service vehicles home at night. Then to add insult to injury, he said that their will be no more long distance phone call reimbursements for business calls made from employee's homes to customer's homes. Consider it your contribution to the cause!! Since our service routs were quit large some of the service addresses were out side of the local area. This really ticked me off since they still owed me for two months worth of business calls. These phone calls averaged an extra $20 to $30 a month per employee!!!!

The employees were not the only ones getting shafted. All branch managers received a memo from corporate headquarters stating that chemical supply allotments were going to be reduced. They claimed the service technicians were using to many supplies in customers homes. After that week, there was a shortage of chemicals and supplies every week. We were all ordered to water down all of our solutions, use half of the instructed doses, use alternative solutions not even labeled for the target pests. This was a direct violation of Environmental Protection Agency safety guidelines. In some cases, we ended up with absolutely no solution by the end of the week and we all had to go to Home Depot and purchase solutions with our own money. We never got reimbursed but were doing this only out of sympathy and respect to our loyal customers. We felt absolutely terrible about using just plain water in our equipment. The management would say "If you were using the chemical-properly, it would last!" "You have to make due until the next shipment of chemical supplies!" Yet the customer was paying for a service that was not being delivered!!!! However, we were in a catch 22. the management told us we had to use something, even though the supply room was empty, but we could not use store bought products. If we were caught with non-company products in our service trucks we were written up and could be terminated and fined. What the hell were we supposed to do????

By now employee turn over was un-godly with only myself and two other original veterans out of 14 servicemen. Every three days somebody would walk out the door frustrated and in disgust. The customer complaints went through the roof. The pest problems only got worse. Customers complained about having a new serviceman every month and that appeared not to know what he was doing. Company policy indicated that every technician was to go through an extensive training program. I did!!! Now they were being thrown out usually on their second or third day of employment to perform un-supervised services in customers homes. The equipment started to fall apart and represent a chemical hazard to the employees and customers. I had a piece of equipment used to dust attics, that I had mentioned multiple times to the management that was leaking seriously! I was only told the company had no funds to repair it, just to use it the way it was or put tape wherever it leaked. One time it literally exploded in a customer's home sending a giant cloud of toxic dust all over me and the customer's home!! I had to evacuate every body in the home and run to a hose and hose myself off. I had to then call the accident in to management to arrange bio-hazard cleanup "so the company procedures called for." I was only ordered to use the customer's vacuum cleaner and take care of the problem. No federal agencies were ever called and it was never reported. A direct and deliberate violation of federal safety laws dealing with hazardous chemical spills. I was the only one to get written up! I was issued a company disciplinary order stating reason for disciplinary action was use of company equipment in an unsafe manner!!! The other piece of equipment seriously neglected was the safety of our service vehicles, such as, brakes, tires, lights and auxiliary equipment mounted on the trucks to perform exterior perimeter treatment of customer's homes. Some trucks were running around with no brakes. We were in many cases ordered to spend our own money for small repairs to the equipment. We were told not to expect a reimbursement just consider it your contribution to the company! This pissed me off!!! I had to spend $20 for a new head light and some turn signal bulbs. We had managers fabricating equipment parts for sprayer machines out of old car parts, discarded equipment, cardboard boxes, or spending their own money at local hardware stores. The sprayer on my truck had a cracked and leaking hose. I had brought it up multiple times at company meetings only to be told there was no authorization from corporate headquarters for repairs. I was then sarcastically told to use some duct tape!!

Just when you thought it couldn't get any worse, all of the employees uncovered a pay scam. The sales representatives were not receiving all of their commissions. This company being merged with one of America's largest home security firms, offered bonuses for cross marketing leads. If I sold a home security system to a pest control customer, I would receive a $50 bonus. I had made a bundle on these bonuses in the past. We would also receive a $30 bonus for any lawn spray leads that sold. However, since the restructuring, my bonus checks stopped rolling in as well as those of the other co-workers. I thought that was very fishy, since some of my customers were sold on the home security systems. They received an excellent discount for being a pest control customer. When I called headquarters in

Atlanta to check up on my leads, they would claim the leads never resulted in a sale. I began a campaign of keeping track of all of my leads. When I would return to the customer's home on the next visit I would just ask them. Well wo and behold, three out of five customers had bought the security systems!! Now I was seeing red! I would call the headquarters after explaining the problem to the customer, right from his home. They would again say that "there was no sale and the lead was still open." I would laugh and say "there must be a mistake, I am standing in the customer's home looking right at the security system and the sales receipt." They would fumble for words and transfer me to some big shot. He would again say "how can we pay you for a lead that's not showing up in the computer as having been sold?" I would reply saying, "speak to the customer he's right here!" "By the way, I want my $50!!!!!!"

I repeated that scenario two more times from customer's homes putting the customer up to vouch for me. Again, I was told the leads had not sold and I was not going to get paid. One long loyal customer of mine respected me so much, he told corporate headquarters if his service man didn't get his bonus, they can have their security system back. oh! boy!, that brought down the house that day! When I returned to the office that day, my supervisor said he wanted to see me in his office. He claimed that corporate headquarters had received two phone calls that day from irate customers. The complaints were on my work performance, attitude, unsafe habits and unsafe use of company equipment. I tried to get the names of the customers, but was told that it was confidential, since the customers were transferred from my rout to another at their request.

Well, the next, day I reported and went about my service calls as usual. At about mid-day, I received a message on my pager. It was my supervisor claiming that headquarters had received more phone calls from customers on my performance and attitude. He said he had to speak to me when I returned. I got a qweezy feeling in my stomach at the tone in his voice. Upon returning, I asked him what the deal was! He said, "finish my paper work and bring all of my books up to date, then come and see me!" I was kind of bewildered but went ahead and did my duties. Well, the time came to find out what was up. He said with a nice tone of voice he has never seen such a diligent hard worker, under the circumstances and was honored to work with me. He said he was ordered by corporate headquarters to let me go! He had a long talk with them to convince them otherwise, but to no avail. He took my paperwork, rout binders and the keys to my truck. While he escorted me out to my car, he commented, "I don't believe them in Atlanta, you would never do the things they accused you of doing!" "Whatever happened, you must have really rocked the boat!"

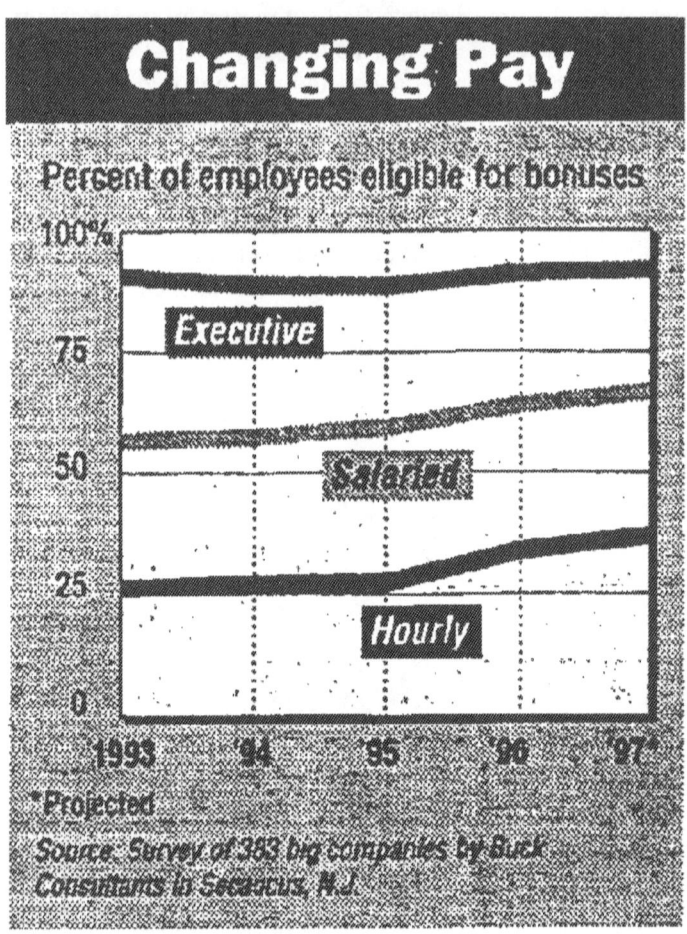

Changing Pay

Percent of employees eligible for bonuses

Executive

Salaried

Hourly

100%
75
50
25
0

1993　'94　'95　'96　'97*

*Projected

Source: Survey of 383 big companies by Buck Consultants in Secaucus, N.J.

"Why More People Are Battling Over Bonuses" By Joann S. Lublin Staff Reporter of The Wall Street Journal Wednesday, January 8, 1997. More people are eligible for bonuses, but are they getting what they have earned? Amidst record corporate profits, one would think bonuses would be booming as well. Ironically that is not the case. "leaving bonus awards to bosses discretion can open the way for conflicts by making pay amounts more subjective. Moreover, at a time of booming corporate profitability, "people have a

very, very high expectations for very high bonuses",
Observes compensation consultant Alan Johnson. At the
same time, he asserts, "on the employer side, there's just
more toughness and meanness over paying earned bonuses,"
"Mr. Johnson managing director of Johnson Associates in
New York, has received 10 requests to act as an expert
witness in bonus related cases during the past year. "A few
years ago, we got none," be ads." "Five years ago, New York
lawyer Jeffrey L. Liddle handled between 100 and 200 bonus
disputes. Today, he says, "we probably have four to five
times as many [bonus] cases a year."

[Illustration 24]

Well one knows a smear campaign, when he sees one! I was
never so upset before in my life! It seemed I got too nosy for
their comfort, as to what happened to my bonuses. If that clearly
was not human exploitation, corporate imperialism or economic
totalitarianism, then I don't know what is! You can bet who ever
thought of that re-organization plan is making the equivalent of
some entire countries national reserve in pay raises and bonuses.
Wake up America, no wonder this corporation is destined to be
on of the top $billion corporations by the year 2000! The
employees are practically working for free and literally paying
them for the honor of working under the glorious name of _ _ _ _
_ . Oops! I am not at liberties to mention names!

I said to myself, "Revenge is a delicacy best served cold!"
And with those words 1 vowed to make their lives miserable. I
knew right where to hit them! Since the reorganization, the
service vehicles and power application equipment were
neglected mechanically and in shambles. The company no longer
practiced proper disposal of chemical run off both in the
chemical room and where the service vehicles filled up. I called
every federal authority I could think of. I had a field day on the
phone.

I notified the Dept. of Transportation (D.O.T.) for the unsafe
service vehicles, giving them exact details on which trucks were

in an unsafe condition. I called the Dept. of Agriculture, telling them where to look for the improper storage and disposal of chemicals and toxins. I contacted the Occupational Safety and Health Administration (O.S.H.A.) for the unsafe leaking application equipment and non-functional safety gear. I phoned the Dept. of Labor, giving details and witnesses, for the pay scam. I called the Dade county consumer affairs, with customer witnesses, for the shady business practices offered to the paying public. I couldn't have been more thorough.

I followed up roughly a month later, giving the federal agencies enough time to close the gauntlet around the un-suspecting mega corporation. Upon making my calls, I was surprised to here that the company had been cited for multiple violations, opening up further inspections of branch offices nation wide. Ahhhh!! Oh how sweet revenge could be! I was on cloud nine! The last time I felt this good was the day I married my wife. I called up one of my co-workers, still employed there, to verify. He said the inspectors were like a swarm of hornets for a couple of weeks.

I gave the authorities a couple of months to process the violations, then I followed up. But fate must have had other plans for me. I called up all of the agencies involved, only to find out I must have stepped foot into The Twilight Zone! One of the agencies claimed the file on the company turned up missing and had no choice but to drop all charges. Another agency claimed to know nothing about the case and the inspector that I identified as doing the inspection never worked there before. Yet another claimed to have been ordered by their superiors in Washington D.C. to no longer pursue the case, and no more information was available. Still another said there was not enough proof to charge the company and dropped all charges. I was utterly shocked!! The company came out of this sqweeky clean and the violations will go on indefinitely.

I seriously under estimated the power of the corporate juggernaut and the influence of the bribe. I analyzed the situation comparing it to similar cases I have seen on T.V. and learned from my mistakes. You can' t, single handed take on a mega corporation of this magnitude and expect justice!! They have too much political clout in domestic, national and international affairs. Most importantly, you must unite with as many fellow employees as possible. Society is more receptive to several people identifying a problem than just one person. Then go public shining the spot light on them in as many ways as possible. You can do this by writing or calling T.V. shows like Inside Edition, Dateline, Sixty Minutes, ABC News, etc. These bad press professionals will work with you to keep the identity of you and your co-workers a secret, to protect your careers by blacking out faces and altering voices. Writing or calling jointly a political leader such as a state governor or President of the U.S. Even a local news paper will do in large metropolitan areas. This has to be done before contacting the federal authorities. All it will cost you is time stamps and phone calls. Once this has been done, let than have it by calling the federal agencies. A federal agency is less likely to side with a large corporation if half the country smells a rat!!! The one case I had with the pest control company might have turned out differently had I done these steps. I however, used some of these techniques with my wife's case and we got a lot more positive reaction. There is an old saying. "You might loose the battle, but that doesn't mean you have lost the war!"

By late 1994, we ran our credit to the max in a futile struggle to survive. Now we could no longer pay our bills and my spotless credit looked more like a Dalmatian. The bill collectors came in like a flock of vultures. Other members of the family were

"MONEY FLIES" It takes money to make money !
Those who need it least,. get it most, those who need it most,
get it least.

[Illustration 25]

experiencing similar difficulties with some already declaring bankruptcy. The family business on my wife's side, a small mom and pop flower shop, had not seen such slow times in it's 17 year history. The regular customers just do not visit as much and when they do they only buy a fraction of what they used to. They all have similar problems with job security, declining wages and plummets in standards of living. Flowers and gift baskets just aren't a necessity for survival!

It looks as though salaries will continue to drop. I took a look through the computerized Job Information Service (J.I.S.) network at the Jobs and Benefits Service Center U.S. Dept. of Labor. I was totally shocked at how little the American worker is paid these days! I could have been a time machine, as I felt I was looking at pay scales of 15 to 20 years ago. Here are a few examples;

1) A laboratory research assistant with a Bachelor's Degree in science, only paid $400 to $450 a week.
2) A police investigation file agent with a Masters Degree in criminal investigation and a minimum of five years of civil service, only paid $400 per week.
3) Three different positions for aircraft mechanics requiring an FAA airframe and power plant repair license, with experience on Pratt and Whitney JT3D and JT8D turbofan jet engines. . These are the same engines on the Mc Donnel Douglas DC-8, DC-9, Boeing 727 and the Boeing 737 commercial airliners. The position only paid $7.95 an hour. I just don't believe it my self, sometimes, I thought I dreamed it and have to go back and see it again just to make sure. Good lord, I know these guys made at least $18 an hour back in the 1980's. That is a fact, my best friend in Atlanta was an aircraft technician in the early 1980's. He was forced out to become an auto repair technician because of plummeting wages. Feel like hopping on that next flight!!
4) An aircraft head avionics repair technician in charge of a repair team. The prospect had to have an FAA avionics repair license, an Associates Degree in college, and at least five years experience. This guy used to get a few dollars

more an hour than an aircraft mechanic. Starting pay $9.00 an hour!

5) A full time dentist with a Doctorate Degree in the field, only got paid $550 a week before taxes. I used to make that and more in a week at the height of my pest control career! That didn't include my bonuses, if I got them. I thought a doctor got a lot more than that? You better brush those pearly whites!

Another horrible transformation, I noticed while on job interviews and surfing the J.I.S. network, was the requirement of college degrees in fields never requiring them before. Some of these jobs have no reason for advanced education scholarships whatsoever, when a high school degree is more than enough! However, most of these jobs only pay a couple of dollars above the minimum wage. In my research, I found out most of these jobs are still paying the same levels as they did before they raised the requirements to advanced degrees. It seems the only thing that the college degree requirements do is to slow the income plunge or stabilize it at past decade levels. What an insult to our college graduates who have worked so hard to try to better themselves!! I thought that having a college degree guaranteed a hefty pay difference compared to non-degree holders? What's going on here? Did I miss something? Some of these positions now requiring college degrees are considered blue collar labor positions. Some of the descriptions are as follows:

1) A secretarial position, requiring an Associates Degree from an accredited college that only pays $5.00 an hour.

2) Data entry position, requiring an Associates Degree from an accredited college. It pays only $8.00 an hour!

3) A medical nurse position only paying $8.00 an hour.

4) A warehouse supervisor, needing a college degree, only paid $7.00 an hour.

5) A department store plain cloths security officer needing an Associates Degree in college and some law enforcement experience required. This position only pays $6.75 an hour.

6) A uniformed security officer position that requires an Associates Degree in criminology, that only pays $8. 00 an hour.

The list goes on and on! I would not be a bit surprised if a garbage man will soon have to have a degree in sanitation engineering or something!!!!!

Some of the more prestigious blue collar positions, that did not require a college degree, until 3 years, ago are as follows:

1) State health inspectors.
2) Dept. of transportation safety inspectors.
3) Dept. of Agriculture inspectors.
4) Drug enforcement agents.
5) F.B.I. agents.
6) Florida state troopers.
7) Fire code inspectors.
8) Sanitation and safety inspectors.
9) Some fire fighter positions.
10) Even some police precincts are now requiring them for street cops.

It seems the rules got changed in the middle of the game. Millions of middleclass workers, who used to make respectable wages in similar fields, can no longer consider employment in them. The proverbial glass ceiling has been considerable lowered. On my job searches, I have found no more respect for high school graduates than that of a drop out, or somebody without any education at all. Millions of middleclass people will be destined to dead end menial labor, minimum wage jobs and manual labor positions. Some may be un-employable. It is just another way for the corporate elite to get more for less! They are getting college educated personnel for the price of non-college degree workers.

One really knows there is a problem when grandma's social security check is equal to a large percentage of the population's full time salaries! This rapid drop in middleclass personal incomes is taking a serious toll on the family

"THE BIG BREAK OF SOCIETY"   A backward society indeed ! In today's society, it seems the more needy or desperate you are, the more you are kicked! When you can't pay your bills on time, the higher the late charges. When you can no longer afford something, and have to return it to the creditors, the greater the penalties. Yet, the rich or famous are showered with better terms cheaper rates, more pardons, and yes, <u>more breaks!!!!</u>

[Illustration 26]

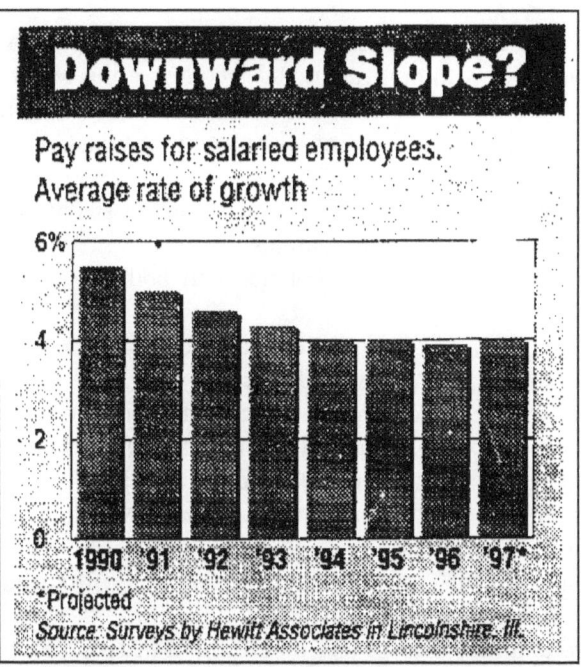

Downward Slope?

Pay raises for salaried employees.
Average rate of growth

6%

4

2

0

1990 '91 '92 '93 '94 '95 '96 '97*

*Projected

Source: Surveys by Hewitt Associates in Lincolnshire, Ill.

"Don't Count on That Merit Raise This Year" By Joann S. Lublin Staff Reporter of The Wall Street Journal Tuesday, January 7, 1997. Says that routine pay increases are headed for extinction. She quotes; "And the raises that are left-which will show up in pay checks in coming weeks-seem to be loosing their punch. Average increases for salaried employees sank to 3.9% in 1996 from 5% in 1990." She also said, "Dial, the big consumer-products maker, last month decided to do away with merit raises for its 1,400 nonunion staffers over the next three years." "But the shift away from the annual merit raise could lower morale and lessen loyalty in an already anxious work force, compensation experts say." Sandra O'Neal, a principal at consultants Towers Perrin quotes; "We are on the precipice of a very big change." She is basically saying that pay raises are a thing of the past, and will not rise with inflation!

[Illustration 27]

75

structure. We are seeing more families with both spouses in the work place, but with non-functional incomes at the poverty line. As these families face fewer resources and become victims of economic dislocation, they must deal with political, social and financial marginalization.

A report done by the U.S. Bureau of the Census has reported the future of most American families.

1) The majority of married couples will both be in the work force.
2) The majority of single parent families with preschool age children will be working full time.
3) There will be more families without children than with.
4) One out of five children will be born to an unwed mother.
5) More than half of all black children, one third of all Latin children and one fifth of all white children will live with one parent.
6) A shocking 60% of all American children will spend some time in a one parent household.
7) More couples, than in any other period in recorded history, will live apart to satisfy work responsibilities.
8) More than half of all marriages started after the 1980, s will end in divorce. It is a miracle my wife and I are still married! Things aren't the same after loosing everything you have worked so hard for.
9) As incomes continue to decline and the cost of living rises, there will be a record number of single family houses with two or more families living together. As they pool their financial resources to survive, we will see the American society of tomorrow more closely resemble that of a third world nation. If the American people have a shred of self respect left in them, they will not allow this unearthly trend to continue!

Kathrine Newman describes the experience of the downwardly mobile middle-class, quoting: "They once had it made in American society, filling slots from the affluent blue collar jobs to professional and managerial occupations. They have job skills, education, and decades of steady work

76

experience. Many are, or were home-owners. Their marriages were (at least initially) intact. As a group they savored the American Dream. They found a place higher up the ladder in this society and then, inexplicably, found their grip loosening and their status sliding. Some downwardly mobile middleclass families end up in poverty, but many do not. Usually they come to rest at a standard of living above poverty level, but far below the affluence they enjoyed in the past. They must, therefore, contend not only with financial hardship but with psychological, social, and practical consequences of "falling from grace, of loosing their proper place in the world" (Newnan, 1988:8).

STAR VEX" Today, the middle-class lifestyle is being bombarded from all directions. With so many negatives, coupled with the increased work load and time taxing responsibilities at work for both husband and wife, the structural framework of the American family is buckling. Today's parents have a fraction of the time to spend with their children compared to a few decades ago. There are more latch key children coming home to an empty house, having to fend for themselves until the parents get home from work. With shrinking pay checks, today's parents can not afford proper day care. Our children aren't getting the proper family support since the parents are too busy struggling to make ends meet. Family values are being thrown out the airlock into the vacuum of space. Under such a massive barrage, it's a galactic miracle the American family is still intact!!

[Illustration 28]

This downward mobility of ninety percent of the population is literally shredding the fabric of American society. Self confidence, self worth are connected directly with career and social status. People tend to blame themselves as their standard of living decreases. Family turmoil will become the norm. Psychological cases and suicide statistics will skyrocket. I was almost a suicide statistic myself, as I started to blame myself for the loss of the American Dream. Crime statistics will continue to rise, as more and more people face fewer economic resources. As they see no hope for the future, people will justify terrible acts of crime against society as their last attempts to retain a functional standard of living. I, myself, can vouch a clean record and consider myself a citizen adamantly against crime. However, when I come home from a long day's work, the refrigerator is empty, my wife is hungry, and my daughter is crying because she is tired of eating rice with left over beans, or a potato with bread, even I have been seriously tempted. Here is an example of a contemporary criminal's justification. "If Clayton hadn't died and I had followed him up the ladder of drug dealers, really being up there for me would have been owning maybe five to seven little businesses, like shirt shops, Laundromats, cleaners...At one point, I was selling ten to twelve thousand dollars worth of narcotics every three to four days, and I had people working for me.... The higher you get up the ladder, the more opportunity you get to stay out of the limelight and get the money at the same time. I always thought of myself as being a hustler. I came from a hustling family. My grandfather told me, when you hustle, what you're really hustling for is so that you won' t have to hustle later.... I ain't never wanted to be real, real rich, but I want to live instead of just survive.... I really think there's a lot of similarity between the people who live out in the middleclass neighborhoods and the people I know. What do most people want out of life? Fun, to be successful, whether it is legal or illegal. Everybody wants to have their own joint... and have two cars. It's just that we are going about it in a different way." Source: Adapted from John Allen, Assault with a deadly weapon: The autobiography of a Street criminal, Diane Hall,

Kelly and Phillip Heymann, eds. (New York: Pantheon Books, 1977),pp. 231-232.

Here is a little more proof that the line between right and wrong will be crossed by more individuals, as more normally law biding citizens are backed into a loosing, no win socio-economic corner. Natural instinct takes, over when one find that the socially acceptable and conventional methods of providing for his family prove to be insufficient. Like a usually submissive animal with babies when it is cornered it can become a violent killer. Even the most righteous citizen will eventually succumb to crime as an absolute last, and final attempt to survive.

Robert Merton offered an explanation, as to the reason economically burdened individuals commit more crimes. He explained society determines our values. It determines the appropriate goals to successfully acquire wealth and the acceptable means to achieve these goals. As a larger number of people are denied access to these goals, and are stripped of all means of attaining them, they will resort to more deviant behavior to achieve them. Criminal deviance is an adaptation people take when society can no longer provide means to the goals. Mc-Gee states deviant adaptations in his analysis of Merton's theory. "The individuals are behaving as they have been taught by their societies. They are not sinful learned or weak individuals who choose to deviate. They are doing what they are supposed to do in order to earn the rewards which their society purports to offer it's members. But either because their positions in the social structure do not permit them access to the means through which to seek the rewards they have learned to want or because the means do not guarantee goal attainment, they become frustrated and experience loss of self-esteem. In a final attempt to do what they have been taught they must, they engage in what is called deviant behavior. Such behavior is simply an attempt to gain the same self-esteem which others are presumed to have and which the society has made it intolerable to be without" (Mc Gee, 1975: pp. 211-212).

It certainly seems that criminal deviance will increase proportionately to the drop in the standard of living in America!

Let's take another peak at the two contrasting perspectives sociologists use to define criminal deviance in our society. The Order Perspective defines cause of criminal deviance in a fashion most likely to be adopted by those in power, and the wealthy upper-class. The Conflict Perspective takes a more sympathetic approach usually adopted by individuals who are financially and socially suppressed. The table I provided for you makes it simple to compare the two perspectives side by side. You can see the contrasting beliefs as viewed from two totally different socio-economic classes.

Order Perspective	**Conflict Perspective**
1) Who is deviant? Those who break the laws of society.	Those who break the rules, but also those who make the rules. Deviance is by the wealthy and powerful, who make the rules. Enactment and enforcement of these rules by the wealthy and powerful assures control of the masses, preserving status quo, and their interests at the expense of those being dominated.
2) The causes of criminal deviance People are criminal deviants because they have not accepted and weren't taught to obey the laws of society.	Deviance is caused by a society which makes the rules which cause deviance. The society causes the behavior that the powerful and wealthy define as deviant.
3) Solutions for criminal deviance. Deviance is controlled with punishment and rehabilitation of criminal deviant individuals through therapy, behavior modification and incarceration.	Deviance is controlled by restructuring society, eliminating insufficiencies by providing higher paying jobs, more help for the needy and a fairer system of justice not biased and reflects the interest s of all groups.

Of course, we all know there are other factors that contribute to crime not associated with Socio-economic status. There are psychological causes, chemical imbalances, child up-bringing causes and peer pressure. But, in reality, Socio-economic factors tend to make up the main bulk of crime statistics. The facts tend to show that the rich, powerful, or famous aren't punished to the full extent of the law. In some instances these high profile individuals are offered special deals or get off the hook all together. Due to my personal experiences, and sociologists theories, this book has been leaning more heavily toward the conflict theory.

Corporate crimes are one of the hottest subjects addressed by me, and the Conflict Theorists, and is used to justify our sometimes radical standpoints. Corporate crimes are more likely to go un-punished, and ignored by the Order Theorists, who label crime as being committed by the lower-class street criminal. In some cases, the vast crimes committed by the wealthy corporate overclass are not even addressed by the Order Theorists. To them, "that is just big business!!" Since most of our family, friends and co-workers have become victims of corporate crimes many time over, I will have to support them whole-heartedly on this subject!

Corporate crime is basically defined as the "illegal and/or socially harmful effects that result from deliberate decisions made by corporate executives in accordance with the operative goals of their organizations " (Kramer 1982:75). You can also bet 100%, that most corporate crimes are committed by corporations in their relentless effort to save money, and raise profits at all costs. The American corporation treats corporate crimes as standard procedures/necessary goals of the company, and the helpless victims as the cost of doing business in America. Some corporations actually plan on and factor in legal fees, fines, damage repair and penalties etc. as part of the company's overhead expenses.

To support the conflict theorists, based on facts gathered everyday watching news reports, reading local papers, personal experiences and sociological studies, it has been proven corporate crime does the largest amount of social, economic and physical damage to society! Further research has proven that the wealthy corporations have a higher crime statistic than do individual citizens. For example, a study of the top 1,000 largest and most powerful corporations found that 11% were convicted of at least one criminal act over a ten year period (Ross, 1980).

Here is what Simon and Eitzen have said, "Imagine for a moment between 1970 and 1979, 11% of the adult population of the United States had convicted of some illegal offense and sentenced to prison. As a result, approximately 12 million people would be placed in a prison system that is overcrowded with a mere half million inmates. At such point liberals and conservatives alike would call crime an epidemic-an institutionalized phenomenon in the U.S. society. However when the same level of corporate crime is discussed, the problem is not considered to be serious" (Simon and Eitzen, 1993:358). You can bet you're bottom dollar that these percentages of corporate crimes are much higher now in the 1990's, with a decade or more of corporate deregulation behind us, than back in the 1970's.

Socially harmful behaviors are also performed by the wealthy corporations as these two conflict theorists explain, "what about selling proven dangerous products (i.e. pesticides, drugs, or food) overseas when it is illegal to do so within the United States? What about promoting an unsafely designed automobile such as the Ford Pinto? Or, what about being excessively slow to promote safe work environment for workers?" (Timmer and Eitzen, 1989:85).

As my readers, let me ask you, whom do you think are the real criminals in modern American society? It was so ironic that, as I was writing this part of the book, South Florida experienced one of the worst aviation disasters in American history. The crash of Value Jet flight 592 into the Florida's Everglades. This opened up a hornets nest of F.A.A. violations being committed by various airlines, shipping companies, freight companies and aircraft repair companies. Yes!, you can bet most if not all of the violations were directly of indirectly related to the fact that corporations were trying to save a buck or two at the expense of the public's safety and well being! Again, it seems the "greed factor" is more important than the "safety factor"!. I then began to think about that $7.95 an hour aircraft mechanic, with experience on the Pratt & Whitney turbofan engines, the same engines on that ill-fated flight 592. Do you, as my readers, think that an aircraft maintenance technician that is being paid $8.00 an hour, a couple of dollars more than a kid flipping burgers at a fast food joint, really cares about the quality of his work since he knows he is grossly underpaid???. This position used to carry an hourly pay of at least $18 an hour back in the 1980 s. You get what you pay for, at least the corporate leaders should have already figured that one out by now!.

With the stepped up F.A.A. investigations, they discovered unqualified technicians, ill-equipped aircraft repair facilities, and improper maintenance logs designed to deceive safety authorities, in the nation's airline corporations. Aircraft were reported flying with holes in the engines even after flight crews had reported them to supervisors. Aircraft were documented flying with loose windshields long after being reported by the flight crews. Some were caught flying with serious hydraulic leaks long after the flight crew had reported the problems, and nothing was ever done. Airlines were found purchasing cheap un-approved parts for airliners. Airplanes were found taking off with intentionally miss-labeled hazardous materials on board, to save a dollar or two. This sounds so familiar, like when I tried multiple times to get vehicles and equipment repaired, at the various places I have worked, only to find myself given every excuse under the sun as to the reason nothing ever got repaired. Most of the time I was ordered to operate the equipment in the un-safe condition, or fired for refusing to operate it!. Then if an accident did happen directly as a result of the un-safe condition of that equipment, the employee gets blamed for operating the equipment in that un-safe condition, and failing to notify management. It's a catch 22, dammed if you do!, dammed if you don' t!, situation!

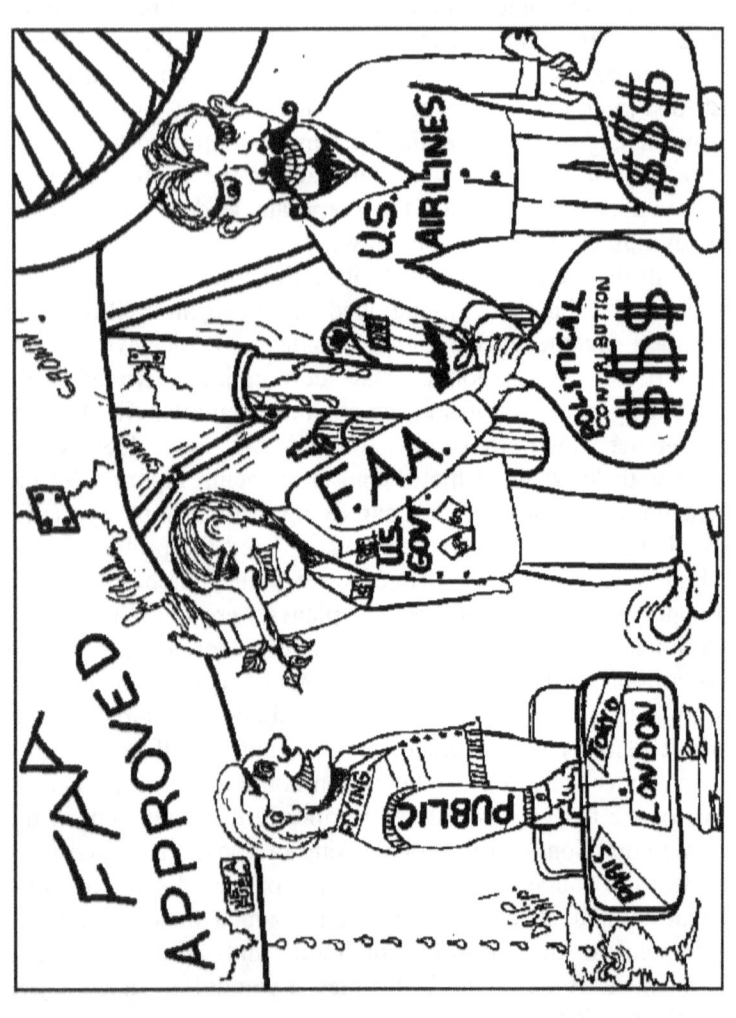

[Illustration 29]

It is bad enough that the wealthy airlines are doing everything in their power to deceive the federal authorities, but what happens when the very agencies designed to prevent these things, are corrupted allowing the violations, that they were created to prevent???. The F.A.A. Federal Aviation Administration, and N.T.S.B. National Transportation Safety Board are created by the federal government to assure safety regulations are enforced and adhered to by the nation's airlines, and aircraft repair facilities. Our lives literally depend on the enforcement of these safety regulations, and the incorporation of newly invented safety equipment into the aircraft. However, the F.A.A. and the N.T.S.B. being branches of the federal government makes them vulnerable to the deceitful political powers of the wealthy corporate airlines.

On May 12, 1997, Channel 7 News, Miami/Ft. Lauderdale had a program called "Uncovering The Truth" narrated by Patrick Frasier. He quoted, "7 News has done it's own investigation probing documents, asking experts from pilots and mechanics, to investigators and investors, to find out if we are safer when we fly. The Answer is NO!" Here is what one chief airline mechanic had to say, "If the flying public knew half of the things that go on, I don't think they would be flying!" An airline pilot had this comment: "If the general public knew some of the things that happen on a day to day basis, I don't think they would fly!"

The Federal Aviation Administration has refused to make improvements across the board for airline safety. They refuse to:

1) Require fire extinguisher installation in all cargo holds!
2) Improve black boxes that monitor pertinent information in case of a crash!
3) Installation of vision equipment to aid pilot's vision in the event of cabin fire smoke!
4) High tech. bomb sensors!
5) Security systems to prevent terrorism!
6) Ban on long work schedules to eliminate pilot fatigue!
7) To improve air traffic control equipment!

Patric Fraiser also un-covered the truth about the supposed passenger cabin oxygen masks over each seat in an airliner. He quotes, "One expert called these the biggest fallacy on the planet. Most of us assume, that when the plane fills up with smoke this will save your life! Wrong!!!!! The air from this mask mixes with the air in the cabin, so if the cabin fills up with toxic smoke, you breath in toxic smoke and die. That's probably what happened to the passenger in the Value Jet crash!" He goes on quoting, "Now the F.A.A. dose require life saving oxygen masks for pilots for military transports, even corporate jets, but they don't require the right kind of masks for passengers on airliners. Why? Take a guess!! Money!!!! The right kind are too expensive!" Bert Werjefeldt an aviation safety expert had this to say. "With de-regulation of the airline industry, came also the de-regulation of safety!" Want to know why the F.A.A. has been so lenient on the wealthy airlines?, political contributions! It turns out three major airlines combined donated $717, 856 the Democratic Party. They also donated $1, 509, 579 to congressional members. Ironically, these donations were timed perfectly, when the White House was looking into methods to make flying much safer! Do you feel like a pawn on a political chess board?? Do you really think the government would bite the hand that feeds them? You figure it out!

Victoria Cunnoch was appointed by the President as an advisor for the Presidential Safety Commission. Her husband John died in the terrorist bombing of flight 103 over Lockerbie, Scottland. She is now a top aviation safety advocate quoting, "Right now, the American flying public is flying less safe, than my husband John was on board Pan Am flight 103!" She is now suing the federal government for trying to silence her from telling the truth, and allowing the airlines to alter Presidential Aviation Safety and Security reports. The airlines claim making airliners safer would cost them too much money! What is the price for human lives? Mrs. Cunnoch quoted "Which plane load of people do you look at and you Mrs. Cunnoch quoted say, you!, you all are going to be the cost of doing business for our airline?" She also says, she is not going to shut up until the White House reveals the truth about aircraft safety. After hearing news of this magnitude, there should be millions of protesters across the nation, picketing airports and marching on the White House!! There should be millions of protest letters in the mail to the leaders of this nation! There should be dozens of talk shows on the subject alone. Sometimes I believe the American people have forgotten how to protest, by speaking their minds and how a democracy really works. Wake up!! America!, how far are we going to let these atrocities go un-answered?

Corporate crime has completely infiltrated our society. It is practiced in just about every corporation from the fast food place down the street, to the local auto dealerships and their service departments. It is apparent the wealthy corporate society has made it standard practice to advertise more and serve less. Basically deception is the rule now, not the exception! How many times have you seen a hamburger advertised on T.V. or pictured on a menu at the restaurant. You see how big and overflowing this delicious sandwich is, so you order one! A minute later you have this yummy delight in you're hand but you notice it doesn't even resemble the picture you see on the wall. It has a fraction of the lettuce and tomatoes on it, and the meat patty is half of the size! "Where's the beef?"

I was having some trouble with the locking mechanism on one of the doors of my car. The other door was just plain hard to open! I recently had the service done at a "supposedly" reputable and popular dealership. I left the car there on the of 5/29/97. I told the service writer to beep me later with the estimate as he couldn't give me one until a service repairman looked it over. He beeped me and I returned his call. The estimate was about $228 to make the repairs on one door. I told him if he couldn't adjust out the hard opening on the other door for about $50 to just fix the one that we couldn't open at all, as he would have gone over our budget! He said no problem!

Upon returning later about 3:30 PM that afternoon, I was told that the car had not been touched, because the parts had not yet arrived, but to wait about 10 minutes as they were on the way. I was promised the service could be completed before 5:00 PM. After about twenty minutes, the parts arrived about 4:00 PM, and I was-notified that the work will begin.

While I was waiting by the cashier in the service islands, I had noticed on two separate occasions irate customers complaining about the amount of time and the labor charges. One gentleman claimed to have left the car there for six hours, but was charged for over 9 hours worth of labor charges at a $59 per hour. He made a big scene saying how crooked this dealership is, but eventually paid the cashier and walked off! The other I couldn't hear exactly how many hours he was overcharged. I then made it a point to check the labor time charges on my bill when I got it. At 5:05 PM I was summoned to report to the cashier as my car was done. The first thing I did was check the number of hours I was charged for labor. I was appalled to find three hours of labor costs, totaling $177 just for labor alone! The grand total was close to $400. The car was only being serviced for about an hour!

I immediately told the cashier I wasn't going to pay for any charges over at the most an hour and fifteen minutes. A supervisor was summoned as my service writer had left for the day. I told the supervisor that there was no way that car was in the shop for three hours! I was here at roughly 3:45 PM and the car had not even been touched because the parts had not arrived. I also reminded him of the estimate and repair parameters, I had laid out while talking to my service writer. He embarrassingly excused himself for about three minutes. Upon his return he said that all repair times are calculated to a standard in a so called Chilton's repair guide for estimating times for various types of repairs. He said, "sometimes a car is repaired in much less time than what is represented in the guide, and the customer is still charged the guide's quote!" So I sarcastically said, "what if a job that requires, let's say 5 hours worth of work, is completed in 30 minutes, does that mean I have to pay for 5 hours worth of work????" He replied yes!!! I then said to him that nowhere on the repair contract does it say that the time used to calculate repair time is not necessarily the actual time in the shop!

He, once again, excused himself for a minute. He returned and said for me to check out all of the service centers with A.S.E. certified repair teams across the nation and they all do this! I replied, "this so called Chilton's service guide is just a legal way for repair facilities to screw the American public and sounds completely illegal", and if those fraudulent charges were not removed, I was going to walk over to that phone and call Carmell Cafiero at Channel 7 News Real Deal, and we will see how legal those charges are!!!!! He looked like he saw a ghost, and excused himself quickly! This time he took 10 minutes to come back. Upon his return, he said, "we have removed all of the extra charges, and printed you up a new bill with some other alterations as well!" This brought the bill down from almost $400 to $296. Upon checking out with the cashier, I gave her three hundred dollar bills, and she gave me my keys and $30 change. I told her the bill was $296 but you gave me $30 change!! She said quickly, "this is for all of the inconvenience we've caused you!"

It seems if you know the name of the local news anchor known for uncovering fraud and corruption and talk the right way, you can quickly defeat any attempt to shaft you!! The sad thing, that really worries me most, is people like the two gentlemen ahead of me, after making a big scene, they still paid the outlandish bills. They gave up so quickly without so much as a fight!! I even walked over and mentioned to the one gentleman, "you should report this place to the consumer affairs or to Channel 7 Real Deal!" He replied, "they don't have time for this stuff, and what good will it do anyway? How many people have been given the shaft, but either they didn't notice, or just said "what's the use of protesting and fighting for the right thing, nothing will be done to stop it!" It seems we have become a bunch of hen pecked, spineless whimps with no guts, and just keep taking the crapp dished out to us!!! How stupid can people be? Sometimes I feel like a lone crusader of virtue, on an impossible mission with all of the odds stacked against me!!

Who are the real criminals? I and my fellow co-workers were forced to work with substandard, leaky equipment, causing a health danger as well as an environmental hazard at my pest control company, then they are caught cheating it's employees out of their hard earned bonuses!

Who are the real deviants? My co-workers and I were forced to drive tractor trailer trucks weighing, in some cases, 100 tons with worn brakes, bald tires, cracked leaf springs or suspensions, worn king pins (the pin that fastens the trailer to the tractor), and in overweight conditions!! Drivers are expected to falsify log books to enable the company to get more mileage out of them. Employees are ordered to get loads from one point to another in a time period impossible to meet, unless they went well over the posted speed limit. All of this in direct violation of D.O.T. safety regulations, and against ones own common sense!

Who are the real criminals? When the employees, who refuse to operate the equipment in that un-safe condition, are threatened with their job security, or outright fired!! And all of this after repeatedly reporting the un-safe equipment to the supervisors to no avail! Then if they choose to risk it for the sake of their jobs, and something does happen as a result of that un-safe situation, the operator gets the blame anyway!

Are the employees, my self included, whom choose the safe rout to be labeled deviants, and get black balled (a term truckers use when they are given a bad work history to keep them out of the industry forever),!

Are the employees criminals because they choose to honor human life, and become un-employed as they are made into trouble makers and turned into examples for the rest of the workers! Again the greed factor seems to be more important than the "safety factor"! Must honor and virtue constantly be repaid with ridicule, discipline and punishment!! Who are the real deviants?? Who are the real criminals??

Liazos has categorized some of the definitions of corporate crime:

1) The unethical, illegal, and destructive actions found in the corporate world, such as robbery through price fixing, low wages, pollution, inferior and dangerous products, deception, and outright lies in advertising.
2) The covert institutional violence committed against the poor by the institutions of society: schools, hospitals, corporations, and the government.
3) The political manipulators, who pass laws, that protect the interests of the powerful and disadvantage the powerless.

4) The power of the powerful is used to deflect criticism, labeling, and punishment even when deserved.

Liazos also quoted: "We should banish the concept of "deviance" and speak of oppression, conflict persecution, and suffering. By focusing on the dramatic forms, as we do now, we perpetuate most peoples beliefs and impressions that such "deviance" is the basic cause of many of our troubles, that these people (criminals, drug addicts, political dissenters, and others) are the real "troublemakers", and, necessarily, we neglect conditions of inequality, powerlessness, institutional violence, and so on, which lie at the base of our tortured society." (liazos, 1972:119)

He states what I have believed all along. We are so busy, bobbing up and down, squawking like a stung parrot, pointing our fingers at the negative results of the problem, instead of concentrating on the real causes, the real threats to our society! We are treating the symptoms instead of the illness.

Ask Your self a question! Do I believe corporate crimes are punished proportionately to the crimes at hand? The answer is probably "In a horse's a _ _ ! It is a fact that wealthy corporations, if they are punished at all, are punished much less than that of a low paid cashier, caught tapping the till, to feed her children, because she is not paid enough to put food on the table, much less keep a roof over their heads. If the cashier is prosecuted, she will probably end up in jail. With no more income, her children will probably be taken by H.R.S. and put into state custody. She will most definitely be evicted from her home for failure to pay the rent or mortgage. Her personal effects will be confiscated or auctioned off to repay any depts. Her car will be impounded, or repossessed. Basically, she will be obliterated! Now on the other hand, the big wealthy corporation will be fined a several thousand dollars, forced to repay any settlements, or to clean up any environmental damages. Basically, pocket change compared to the company's corporate portfolio of several $million to a $billion or more.

Let's even justice a bit in a hypothetical situation, to see equality between the mega corporation and the cashier. A large corporation is caught committing a corporate crime, such as price fixing, stealing from the public, substandard wages, false advertising, environmental destruction, and safety violations resulting in serious injuries or death to an employee, etc. All in an effort to maximize profits. The authorities would move in and handcuff the corporation's ceo and upper management. The workers would be sent home, and the offices would be boarded up. All company equipment would be confiscated, and auctioned off to settle all disputes. All company assets liquidated. Ultimately the building and property would be foreclosed. How often do you here of such cases? Very rarely! I can only recall of one prominent case. The savings and loan scandal in the 1980's. If such justice did really occur, the percentage of corporate crimes would be a fraction of what they are today. It happens more to the mom and pop businesses, and the individual citizens. It happens more to those unable to defend themselves, and put up a valiant fight! Who do you suppose deserves a harsher punishment, the cashier or the corporation?? Do you believe in the conflict theory?

In the face of virtually unpunished corporate crimes, and a deceitful justice system, one would expect street crime to rise. Criminals and potential criminals will see these wealthy, prestigious criminals defy the law, and get even richer doing so. They will literally believe crime really does pay! Or they will totally give up trying to maintain their standard of living, when the conventional way is no longer adequate. They will see crime as the only way left to survive.

Who is ultimately a deviant and whom is given the privilege to hand out the label? Sociologists define the term deviance, not so much as an individual or a community thing, but as the process, by whom in power is creating the process by which certain individuals are singled out, and forced to wear the negative label. The Robin Hood factor! The wealthy and powerful considered Robin Hood a criminal deviant, yet the poor masses looked up to him as a godsend hero. This makes me recall some well noted science fiction movies like Logan's Run, Soylent Green, Blade runner, Demolition Man, Mad Max, Dune, etc. These movies are depicting a future where the normal people, by our standards, are the deviants, and the wealthy deviants in power are the normal people. Thus deviance is more of a perspective thing! Since the basis of all laws and rules in our society are instilled by those in power, and those in power are generally from the wealthy, power elite overclass, deviance would be more directed toward the lower-classes, minorities, poor, powerless, renegades, rebels, vigilantes, dissidents, and any body who dares to challenge the current status quo. By now, I have more than likely been labeled a deviant, that's if you are a member of the corporate elite.

From the conflict theorist's point of view, the wealthy and powerful benefit from the current status quo, and vigorously crush any ideas, individuals, or groups that attempt to reform society to benefit the masses. Thus anybody that makes the overclass the least bit uncomfortable, will be labeled a deviant. I guess you know what that makes me!!

If this book does it's job, shattering status quo, by uniting the masses to the cause of returning some of the wealth in the hands of the corporate power elite, back into the masses, I will definitely be labeled negatively. I may be labeled a dissenter, dissident, non-conformist rebel, and in extreme cases, a Marxist, Leninist, Natzi, or Communist. They will do this in a vigorous attempt to destroy my ideas, my book and my sources in the eyes of the public. This will be their method of attempting to maintain status quo. As a patriotic American, I want to get one thing straight. I am strongly against Communism, Natziism etc. The many goals of this book is to reverse years of social conditioning, and to help the American people identify this terrible abomination that's risen out of wonderful capitalist America, that once gave more people the comfortable, middleclass American Dream. To prevent those puzzled looks, and feelings of despair so many people tend to harbor when they are asked about their mounting responsibilities at work, shrinking paychecks, and their declining standard of living. To alert the citizens of this country to the real socio-economic problems plaguing our standard of leaving and lifestyle. To create enough self esteem in the average middleclass working American, to shatter our worst enemy status quo (which is the belief that there is nothing anybody can do, that's the way the cookie crumbles, that's our destiny, what good is protesting, things won't change, that's life, or I don't have time). To unite the brow beaten masses against a common threat effecting 95% of the American population for the first time since World War II.

As more middleclass families fall from grace into the ravages of poverty, I want to remind them that they are the majority and were given the ultimate power with rights in the Declaration of Independence, the Constitution of the United States, and our founding fathers to unite and preserve our nation. To preserve our government even when it can no longer preserve itself in the onslaught of a common enemy. To say that the people of the United States of America control their own destinies, not a hand full of overclassmen and their families that play with our government like a puppet, manipulate and condition our masses, pillage and plunder our standards of living for their own benefit. To prove that the American people have to unite, stopping this socio-economic raping of a people, and return the American Dream with dignity to the majority, not just the privileged few!!!!

Chapter 5 The buck stops here! What we can do <u>NOW!</u>

It was the spring of 1995, I had literally given up on finding a decent job driving an eighteen wheeler locally. After walking out of several job interviews because of ridiculously low wages, I realized it was futile to find any local jobs paying much over $8 an hour. No way in hell was I going to operate a 65 foot plus semi truck, and all of the responsibilities with it for the same pay rate I was earning 14 years ago driving a small 25 foot cube truck!! I promised myself, if I was going to work for a pay rate from over a decade ago, in a world where the cost of living has more than doubled in the same time frame, it was going to be a very little responsibility job. Nobody gets my services for free! A straight 10 wheel 20 cubic yard dump truck fit the bill just fine.

I started to drive this dump truck for a large prominent South Florida rock and sand company, based in Florida City, between Homestead and the Florida Keys. I was literally hired on the spot at the rock quarry. After all I have the Boeing 747 airliner operator's license of land operated vehicles. I have a Class A C.D.L. with doubles and triples, hazardous materials, and tanker endorsement. I could drive the largest (any number of axles), the longest (two to three forty foot trailers hooked up like a train), and the heaviest (with overweight permits), of all trucks. If it rolled I could drive it! I could carry any kind of, or combination of cargo, from pillows, baby toys, to thousands of gallons of gasoline, and nuclear warheads. This dump truck was barely half of the size the rigs I was accustomed to operating. A typical run consisted of backing under a front end loader, getting thirty tons of rock or sand, and delivering it through out Dade county and the Florida keys. Upon arrival at my destination, I just pushed a few buttons and swishhhh_____ h goes the load out the back door! Nothing to it!

After my first week, I noticed incredible employee turn over. Every couple of days there was a new face and no explanation as to what happened to the old one! Out of thirty some drivers, every body was tight lipped and didn't talk much about anything. I really started to smell a fish, when I notice all of the drivers carried a lunch in their coolers with them. That was strange, after all our runs into the key Largo on US 1 took us past dozens of fast food joints, and 7 11 stores, plus they took an hour out of our pay checks each day for lunch. One day after a run I decided to stop and get a bite to eat. While eating, I noticed a couple of our other trucks go by. Upon returning to the quarry, while waiting for another load, I was approached by one of maybe three senior drivers. He was a humble man with mostly gray hair in his late fifties. He said, he noticed me pulled over along side the road at about 1:00 PM in the Key Largo area. I said, I had stopped to eat lunch and take my hour break. Leaning closer he grunted under his breath and said, "you don't want to get caught pulled over to get lunch, coffee, or to use the restroom!" I immediately said, "why not?, and by the way they take an hour out of my pay every day for lunch!" He quickly blurted out in a loud whisper, "you will get fired, that's why!" "They may deduct an hour but you don't stop working!" These guys would literally work a 9 to 10 hour day, sometimes 6 days a week without taking a single break. They would eat and drive at the same time. If they needed to go to the bathroom, they would go between the tandem wheels, while the front end loader was filling up their trucks for the next run. We all prayed that our trucks were the only ones needing to "take a dump", and number one was our only deposit!

I was just another brow beaten, hen pecked, spineless victim of status quo, and took the old man's advise. Yes, I was mad about giving them a free hour of my labor every day, but I didn't Know what else to do and figured nothing would be done to stop this humiliation anyway!

I finally found out what was happening to most of the drivers. They either quit, but most of them would get fired. There was one supervisor, who took a long sightseeing drive into the keys, almost every day around lunch time for no apparent reason but, to look for drivers pulled over having lunch, coffee, or to use the bathrooms. The old driver told me about him, and how he would catch drivers in restaurants, quick marts, or gas stations. He would come right up to them while they were eating and say he wanted to talk to them when they returned to the quarry. You guessed most of the people would always get terminated just under 90 days before their benefits would kick in. The news paper always seemed to be running job listings for this company. Next victim Please!!!!!

About two months and three weeks into the job, I was accustomed to making sure I did number two at a gas station on my long 45 minute ride into Florida City from Miami. On this morning, I was running late, and did not have time to stop and do my normal routine. The report time was 6:00 AM sharp, and not a minute later! I figured there would be no problem, I will load up my truck, and use the bathroom stalls by the maintenance shop on the way to the weigh scale house to set my gross weight. When I came out, I almost bumped into a supervisor, standing there looking into my eyes. He sternly asked me, the way a father might bark at a child, "What are you doing?" I replied "I just had to use the bathroom!" He sharply said, "You are not allowed to stop!" I kindly replied again, "All I had to do was use the bathroom!" He then firmly quoted, "I don't care, you better learn to control you're bodily functions!" At that moment, a feeling of hot boiling water enveloped me, as my temper flared. I sternly looked him square in the face, and said, "Now you listen here!, if I have to use the bathroom, I am going to stop and use the bathroom!" I cut him short saying, "Every body has the right to use the toilet!" He replied with a calm, "We will see about that!" as he walked away. Well, I was never so upset in my life, but I went about my duties as usual. I kept saying to myself, "This must be some sort of joke or something!" At the end of the day, I stopped by the scale house to see if there was anything else that needed to be done. The guys told me to park my truck, and turn in my paper work, then to see the personnel manager. Well, I knew what was in store for me, so instead of going all the way to the back of the quarry to park the truck, and then have to come all the way back up to the office, I decided to go in now and face the music! He wasted no time and came out and told me, "The company has reviewed you're performance, and has reached the conclusion, that you will not work out for the best interests of the company." I then replied, "This must be because

I stopped to use the restroom this morning, isn't it? He said Yes, and explained that he not have employees stopping to use the toilet, or for any other reasons, or he would not get any production done. I followed by saying "what if you have to go?" He counter replied by quoting, "We are all adults, unfortunately, we have to learn to control our bodily functions!" Before I could say anything else, he quickly said, "I am very busy and I don't have time to debate with you, have a good day!"

I walked back out to the truck and hopped in to take it to the parking lot. As I drove the long dirt road, a whole flurry of life's events rushed through my mind. I parked the truck, and walked into the dispatch office to hang my keys on the hook, and turn in my paperwork. As I turned to walk out, I suddenly thought to myself, "Why make it so easy for them!" There was nobody in the office, because some of the trucks were still out on their runs, while others were already parked for the night, and the supervisor was out driving around the quarry. I looked at all of the keys on the peg board, and said, "why not!" I took every key there and stuffed them into my pocket. I then looked at all of the turned in signed work orders turned in from the other drivers for the day's work, including mine sitting there on top. I quickly stuffed them all back into my metal clipboard, and headed for my car parked by the lake. I reached into my pocket, and grabbed all of the keys throwing them as far as I could out into the lake, following them with the clipboard!

As I drove the long ride home, I didn't take the Turnpike, the usual way home, but instead US 1. I felt as though I was on auto pilot, as an entire lifetime's worth of memories flooded in my mind. I was one of those people who literally accepted things as they were. I would get all angry at these type of things, ultimately blaming myself afterward. I would have many sleepless nights, as I re-played all of the corporate crimes committed to me and my family over and over. I thought of my wife with a new horn baby in her hands, crying endlessly due to her termination at work, because she was given the ultimatum to choose her family or her career, and she chose her family. I thought of my mom, whom after 19 years with a major jewelry store chain, being terminated 14 month before her retirement. She was terminated because her bladder got weak due to age and need for an operation, which required more visits to the restroom than was allowed by the company. I thought that something had to be done, but what? I was always told you have to take the crapp! That's the way the cookie crumbles! There isn't anything anybody can do to stop this. What good is my voice, I am nobody, and nobody cares! I am just a pee on in the grand scheme of things. All of this after a slow humiliating slide from a comfortable middleclass lifestyle, to a sub-poverty, struggling, day by day struggle to survive today. I figured, we just had to adjust to this downward mobility, even if it meant living out of my car under a bridge with my wife and child. As the car drove forward, I was thinking how we just moved again, for the fourth time, not to many

OLDER AMERICANS IN THE WORK FORCE

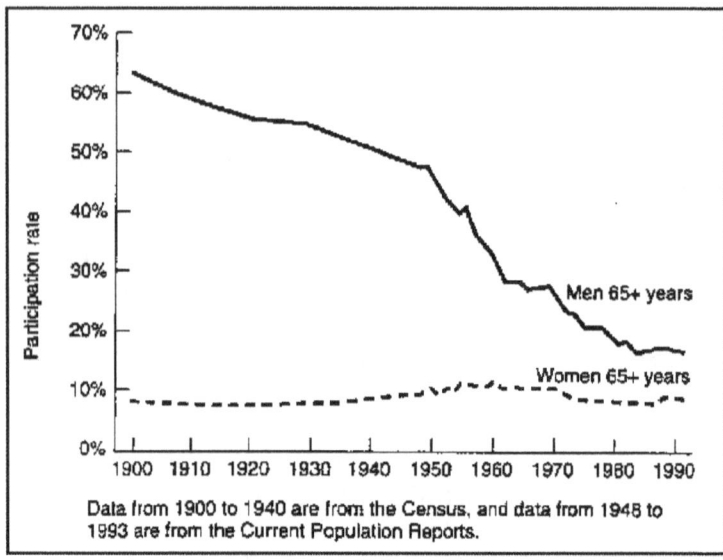

Data from 1900 to 1940 are from the Census, and data from 1948 to 1993 are from the Current Population Reports.

Thrown out with yesterday's news paper. Older men, more so than women, are finding it harder and harder to maintain employment. Even though labor laws forbid age discrimination, corporations openly throw out employees they consider too old for fast paced corporate tasks. If challenged, the corporations claim other un-true reasons for the termination. Like an old race horse, all the labor laws in the land could not prevent these stallions from ending up dog food or glue!

[Illustration 30]

weeks ago to avoid skyrocketing rents. Now I could see the frustration in my wife's face after she hears the bad news! After all of our bad experiences with employers, I now blamed myself more than ever even though deep down in my heart, I knew it really wasn't our faults at all! Now with life in the streets, a possible reality, the fury ran deeper than ever before. We just wanted to be treated like human beings, not like some expendable garbage to be used and dumped without the bat of an eye!

An eerie calm took over as my car drove it's self into the parking lot of a drug store. Like a pre-programmed robot, I bought a whole box of sleeping pills with the last $5 in my pocket. Upon arrival at my home, I took the lethal dosage, and sat down to write a final will with a short letter to my family. As the feeling of tingling numbness all over my body, and the appearance of sparkling lights in the room, I made a quick call to my wife at work to give her and my Adriana all of my love! That's the call that saved my life!!

After this brush with death, and a week in intensive care, like a phoenix rising out of the ashes, a new wonderful out look on life came over me. The rage I once directed toward myself became the fuel to feed a new re-directed anger in a positive direction, to change the seemingly un-changeable. Why should I kill myself and run from the problem? The day will come when the public will no longer be intimidated to just shrug it's shoulders only to say there is nothing that can be done!, That's life!, or some other version of those solemn words of hopelessness. It's time for the powerless, humble and meek to take the bull by the horns, and return the American Dream to the right track to the masses, not the wealthiest few. <u>THE BUCK STOPS HERE!!!!</u> With those words, I will strive to educate the public on methods to overcome status quo, and like David to defeat this terrible Goliath, one day I hope to never see those looks of despair in the faces of the working class again, if it's the last thing I do in this world!

With the new quest, which I pursued like an obsession, I did my home work. I read countless books on sociology, countless articles in modern magazines, to watching news programs and

103

talk shows on the subject of declining standard of living in America. I even performed street interviews of the middleclass population, from all races and back grounds. I discovered that most Americans share the same views I do! The only ones that seem completely content with the current status quo, are the very wealthy corporate elite. I found out there is a lot we supposedly powerless can do. It just took for me to be at the end of my rope for me to see the real truth through the smoke screen called status quo. No more hen pecked, Mr. Nice Guy here! I will never be a victim of social conditioning, and status quo again! This hound dog is not going to continue to sit helplessly on a burr and howl! This dog is getting up and going to do something NOW!!!!

After reading this last chapter, I hope you will analyze you're situation, and join me in taking steps to change the un-changeable to reverse years of social conditioning and status quo. Even, if now you are currently living the American Dream.

We all must never take our American Dream for granted. I thought it would always be there for me and my family. Boy I was wrong!! I surly learned the hard way, and realized it will only be a matter of time before all of us will be come a victim! With our incomes slowly dropping, yet today a trip to the grocery store can be an un-settling, undesirable event for Americans. To walk out with 6 bags of groceries can cost close to $130. That's half of most American's weekly take home pay! In 10 years a two bedroom, one bath apartment has jumped from around $325 a month to about $700 per month. A typical Three bedroom, two bath house has sky rocketed from about $70,000 ten years ago to ¿ un-godly $130,000. A gallon of gasoline is now at an all time high of $1.32. A typical family car has risen to double the price of a decade ago. And our pay checks are half of what they used to be!! Is this my imagination or has the American Dream gotten farther out of reach for the average American????

The birth of America is rooted in discontent, civil disobedience and violence, which ultimately ended up in a revolutionary war. This is the most famous violent revolt of an oppressed people. When the problems, grievances, and insufficiencies from the colonists continually fell on the deaf ears of the king of England, they resorted to civil disobedience, and ultimately violence. This led to the eight years of war known as the American Revolutionary War.

The Declaration of Independence was designed by our founding fathers as a tool to unite an oppressed people against a common problem, and to rationalize mass civil disobedience and finally violence. Listen closely as you read these words of conception of America. I suggest you read than out loud to your self!

"We hold these truths to be self-evident, that all men are created equal, that they are endowed by their Creator with certain unalienable Rights, that among these are Life, Liberty, and the pursuit of Happiness. That to secure these rights, Governments are instituted among Men, deriving their powers from the consent of the governed. That whenever any form of Government becomes destructive of these ends, it is the Right of the People to alter or abolish it, and to institute new Government, laying its foundation on such principles and organizing its powers in such form as to them shall seem most likely to effect their Safety and Happiness. Prudence, indeed, will dictate that Governments long established should not be changed for light and transient causes; and accordingly all experiences hath shewn that mankind are more disposed to suffer, while evils are sufferable, than to right themselves by abolishing the forms to which they are accustomed. But when a long train of abuses and usurpation's, pursuing invariably the same Objective evinces a design to reduce them under absolute Despotism, it is their right, it is their duty, to throw off such Government, and to provide new Guards for their future security".

These are some of the most beautiful words ever written on a piece of paper. They are a also the most powerful rights ever written into law!! This assures, and guarantees that the mass majority yield power over the government, and this government is there to be used by the masses to serve their desires and interests. Therefore, the government is to obey the demands and the needs of the majority, and to assure nothing prevents access to the American Dream!

Being married to a Cuban American, my lovely wife Zenaida, has made me realize that the average American citizen now takes these powerful rights for granted. My wife and her family fled the tyranny of Fidel Castro in the late 60, s. These once oppressed people do not take any civil rights for granted, and they analyze the rights in this country with the utmost scrutiny. They also exercise them more readily, and more diligently than any American I know. The saying, "Can't see the forest because of the trees!" describes the brainwashed American people. Cuban Americans also tend to be less influenced by status quo, and less effected by social conditioning. The elderly members of my wife's family have noticed a terrible and scary trend in this country. The American people do not use the rights their founding fathers have given them. The Cuban people have a higher percentage that vote when elections, and amendments are voted on in the poles. If a new outrageous tax is proposed, they show up in mass to vote it out. They will picket by the thousands and march on federal buildings, if a civil liberty has been abused. If a powerful corporation has done mass corporate crimes to these people they will, publicize, boycott, and picket the business which usually creates immediate results. These people remind me more of the American people of a century ago, when the country was young, and citizens were not afraid to voice their opinion and make speedy changes to right societal problems. They ain't so darn hen pecked!!!

I told you about this because even I being a grass roots American have been put to shame at the patriotism these people show. They still have faith in the American system. I mentioned these things because it leads up to the most important factor we as Americans must overcome, to prevent any further slide in the American middleclass lifestyle. <u>STATUS QUO!!!!!</u>

As Americans, most tend to be un-concerned about the things that effect our every day lives. We are in our own little worlds, oblivious to the things that tear our society apart. We are too quick to just say "What's the use!" "I don't have the time!" "Let somebody else make up our minds for us!" "Let somebody else worry about it!", or some other tuck your tail between your legs, throw in the towel saying. It shows at the poles on election years. We do not show the unity our founding fathers had when this country was born. We have become passive, complacent sheep being led around by those in power. We accept un-contested authority, and un-contested societal insufficiencies. This is very scary because the government, and the wealthy corporate leaders are then in the position to suppress everyone socio-economically. I am beginning to wonder if an enemy form of government such as Fascists, Communists, Natzis, etc. infiltrated our beloved White House, would we just sit back, cowering in fear, and do nothing?

The job is going to be more difficult than ever before to get the problems of declining standards of living addressed. The federal government has become a literal puppet of the rich corporate society. Mind you this rich overclass is by far, not the mass majority, but the smallest minority. The proverbial fox has been given control of the hen house for too long! Now it's going to be harder than ever to evict him! The wealthy corporations tend to set the helpless governments control, and decisions to their disposal. They do this with the ever alluring power of big money. Our government addicted to big money is like a drug addict in desperate need of a fix. Therefore the wants and desires of the rich are usually considered.

Like a cancer patient, the very spirit of America is being drained slowly. This overclass, under the spell of the "Greed Factor", has done more damage, and presents a danger more terrible than any war, person or enemy institution has ever presented in the history of this country. We may very well be witnessing history in the making! The fall of Babylon!! We have nobody to blame but ourselves!!!!

Here is what we can do, but the million dollar question is, how can the literally powerless change a biased system, if they lack the power to do just that? Why don't we ask the corporate elite to take a pay cut back to the levels they made 15 years ago, so they can pay their employees more enabling the workers to live the American Dream again! Yeah right!! No way!, they are so used to seeing constant growth in their personal standard of living, even though 10-15 years ago they made more than enough to live in luxury. They would not tolerate a pay cut of any kind! They are a victim of their own so called "Greed Factor". The more they make, the more they live it up, the more they want, therefor, the more they have to make to satisfy the ever growing addiction. This is a terrible sickness, similar to drug addiction, compulsive gambling, compulsive shopping, or any other form of Psycho-compulsive disorder.

Here are two across the board forms of positive actions the supposedly powerless masses can take to address a large scale problem, that are socially acceptable:

1) Protest in as many ingenious ways as you can. This is usually done though writing letters to public officials, and decision making powers, petitioning and voting on persons and bills that directly effect the problem or cause in which you support.

2) The second step is a slightly more stern posture, with a more impolite resolve, yet socially acceptable. This is done by loud but peaceful demonstrations, marches, picket lines in public places, and boycotts. These first two methods are commonly utilized by labor unions to protest employee rights violations, or get legislation that benefits employees. The first two should also be done by the individual citizen, as well as the labor unions. This way the labor unions cover the particular problem from their angle, and the individual citizen covers the problem on a more personal level. Public officials are more likely to take notice and address a grievance, if the protests come in from two different directions. This shows the large scale impact the particular problem is having on society. This is like a one-two punch! If you really want action, and you happen to be a union member currently, you should also protest on a personal level to the same officials. The tactics mentioned in this second step are an attempt to draw as much public and media attention as possible.

3) The third step is the last resort, when all else has failed. The common forms of protesting in this last effort, consists of civil disobedience, threats, violent marches, riot protests,

guerrilla tactics, and ultimately civil war! These methods are usually not socially acceptable. These methods are also frequently miss-directed causing harm to innocent people and property.

If one pays any attention to national events these days, he will realize there has been a sharp increase in the number of anti-government dissident groups, terrorist attacks, Communist groups, skin heads, and Ku Klux Klan activities. We have seen terrible acts committed against innocent men, women and children. i.e. Oklahoma federal building bombing, the Freeman anti-government group in Montana, and the Branch Davidian Waco Texas incident. People don' t always direct their energies in the right directions, as well as the personal gains and greedy intents of the groups leaders cloud their judgment. However miss-directed and twisted these incidents seem, these are the warning of a more serious problem in American society. This means that people are feeling more discontented with the current system. Unfortunately, history and the very nature of mankind has proven there will not be a peaceful transfer of financial resources and power. The haves will do whatever it takes to thwart the efforts of the have nots. Being led by greed, the haves will use their tremendous political clout to convince the military and law enforcement authorities to impose martial law to protect their interests at all costs. If sociologists are doing their jobs, they will realize we are headed for disaster!

This is my concern, as more middle-class people experience down ward mobility, and become borderline poverty, they will make desperate decisions. The enemy political powers of the world know that desperate masses often are vulnerable to propaganda, and make choices not beneficial in the long run. They do this to prevent further suffering. Therefore it's our patriotic duty, as Americans, not to fall into a false sense of security with any of these anti-government, or alternative political powers. Being Americans we are already members of the most powerful politically, and societal altering group on the face of the earth. As a group united our vote is the most powerful law in the universe. Therefore we have no need to join any other groups or allow ourselves to be led by fanatical political leaders. As a united front, the American peoples demands will not be halted, even by the mighty overclass!

Again, the reason this greed factor has gotten out of control, is you and I. Since we, of all national origins, men and women, and all educational backgrounds, were children, we have more or less been taught (brainwashed) into accepting societal negative trends such as unfair, unequal insufficiencies, biased distribution of wealth and power, no matter how detrimental they are to us. On my street interviews, I am totally shocked at how many people are victims of status quo. Over 90% of the people I have interviewed share the same feelings. They have said: "There is nothing we can do!", "That's our destiny!", "We will just have to live with it!", "We are helpless!", "The rich will always get richer, and the middleclass and the poor will always get poorer!", "That's life!", "That's the way the cookie crumbles!", "We are nothing but peeons, and have no real power to change things for the better!", "What's one little voice going to do?", "Oh well if you don't have money nobody cares!" Wake up America! This is exactly what the wealthy and powerful are banking on! You can literally bet they are taking it to the bank by the truck loads. We are playing right into their game.

With attitudes like this, it's a miracle the American Revolution, and the birth of the United States ever occurred! Our founding fathers must be doing somersaults in their graves. For the sake of God and country, this social condition factor must be defeated. This is ultimately going to be the most difficult hurdle. This factor alone will make or break the future quality of life, the middleclass, and the American Dream for the majority. We are afraid to ask for raises when one is surely deserved. We sit back as the American Dream fades away with our bank accounts. We watch helplessly as the repo man takes our cars because we can no-longer make the payments. We get evictions and foreclosures on our homes ending up homeless, because our standard of living no longer allows us to maintain mortgage or rent payments. We will ultimately watch the death of the American Dream for the vast majority of the population. All the while the powerful overclass will get wealthier. The champagne corks will fly, more larger mansions will be built by under paid workers, more yachts will sail, more Rolls Royces will be parked in their garages. Guess what?,– they think they won't have to lift a finger to silence our voices. They believe the battle will be won, before it will ever be fought. As for me, it will be a snowy day in hell before I will live in a ghetto, and watch the American Dream slip out of reach for me and my children!

<u>We have to do something now!!</u> MY fellow Americans, we know the American capitalist system works. In the past more Americans lived the American dream, we were there! This wealthy corporate elite has it's rightful place in the grand scheme of things. Like the worlds greatest most powerful predators, such as the Great White sharks in the seas, the great cats, the mighty North American Grizzly on the land, and the powerful swift birds of prey in the skies, we must not exterminate them. For without this corporate overclass, the American Dream could have never been lived. As I have stated earlier in this book, we are witnessing capitalism at it's worst extreme. The old saying "To much of a good thing is a bad thing", is so true. As we have seen in the past regulated capitalism is the best thing. Like a mothers wayward child, the government can be our best friends again. The government is what we make it, and we must help it back on to it's feet. We must support existing watch dog agencies, and create new agencies to police the corporate scene. These policing agencies will guarantee fairer, heftier fines for corporate crimes, fairer humane treatment of the American employee and consumer, both financially and physically. The message is "you do the crime you do the time!" Unfortunately, under the last several administrations, the fox has been given charge of the hen house for too long, and has had a finger licking good picnic.

Support all legislation and efforts to raise the minimum wage. Write letters to public officials, and political figures pushing for a dollar or more, not just 25¢ or 50¢. Minimum wage has by no means kept up with inflation.

The next request is going to be the hardest for the average American citizen. No matter how difficult this is, it must be done to turn the tides in our favor. The next job interview you are on and the employer quotes you a ridiculous wage, well under the pay rates for comparable jobs in the past, look him square in the eye and say, "Would you work for that?", "I can't support my family on those wages!", "Could you support your family on those wages!" You must be firm!!! If you aren't given a fairer review, shake his hand and wish him luck on his search and walk out. Being a pioneer is by no means an easy task. I have done this several times, even though I knew I was desperate and needed a job as soon as possible. We must not let others undercut our attempts to raise as many peoples standards as possible, by settling for substandard wages. This is the most important message you as citizens united can send corporate America. We will not work for less!!!!

Living here in South Florida there is a large supply of immigrants, new to this country, whom are ignorant. They are willing to work for substandard wages with out any questions. They don't know any better, because in their third world countries, minimum wage would make them very wealthy. Therefor, the illusion of financial security is very real to them, as they have never earned that much money before in their lives. By American standards they will not survive. A large segment of their population is forced to be on welfare even though they are working full time and in some cases more than one job. They are forced to live with multiple families in single family homes, with one maybe two cars as they pool their resources to survive. However, this trend is starting through out grassroots America as well as the standard of living keeps falling.

We are seeing children leaving the nest much later in life, as they are finding it harder to make it on their own. We have young adults with families moving back in with mom and dad because they have gradually lost their proper place in society. We must educate these immigrants to their real potential in the American Dream, and raise their expectations up with ours.

Wages across the nation have stagnated, or have dropped considerably, however here in South Florida middleclass wages have declined faster than the rest of the nation's. For example, the $7.95 an hour aircraft maintenance technician, the $450 a week dentist, the $250 a week tractor trailer operator, the $300 a week legal secretary, the commuter airline pilot working for bus driver's wages, the $7.00 an hour electrician, plumber, carpenter with his own van and tools, just to name a few. Because people are willing to accept these ridiculous wages, the American income standards/status quo, and the standard of living of all Americans are being permanently re-adjusted for the worst.

Support and/or join labor unions wherever possible. The labor union is the greatest guardian of the common working masses. They are the most powerful political bargaining chip for the working class in the world of lobbying. They literally set corporation s working standards for the benefit of the employees. Union jobs pay much better, and have the least employee turn over. Union jobs have better benefits, and have the safest working environments of any work place. Unfortunately, under the last few presidential administrations, the unions have taken a hell of a beating. Corporations practice union busting, and are constantly pushing federal, state, and local governments to make life hard on them. If your state is a non-union state, write letters to the governor and the senator to get the unions back to their fullest potential. We must convince state and federal governments, that unions are the only large scale counter balancing force between the common workers and the wealthy corporate world of the overclass. The unions must be returned to the grandeur and respect they once had. No excuses, like "I don't want to pay union dues!" Even with these dues, the working American will make a hell of a lot more money than without. The worker will come out way ahead of non-union workers. The advantages far outweigh the disadvantages. I have tried on countless occasions to have a union job, but have found out there are not enough of them to go around, and you virtually have to have a relative already there to help you get in. Competition is fierce. People just don't leave them, and the only positions are available when somebody retires or moves.

Some states adopt policies that are seriously biased to favoring the rich corporations, at the expense of the working American. These states are known as "right to work" states. Florida is a right to work state. These policies basically give the wealthy ceo's and the corporate policy makers more freedom to legally take advantage of the employees, both on the financial and the worker safety arenas. In right to work states, federal and state labor laws have no teeth in them, therefore the corporate crimes can go on literally un-punished. Discrimination cases of all types carry much less weight in the court room. Corporations can literally fire you because you get sick, pregnant, they don't like the color of your hair, eyes, or they don' t like your mother. Corporate policy makers can impose, otherwise un-ethical standards and rules in the work place. My bathroom incident was one! And my mother's restroom incident was another. Even the family leave laws in Florida carry little weight as me and my wife have found out pursuing our case. It was only after we made a big stink all the way up to the White House, that the case got the respect it deserves. Florida's "right to work policies", have caused a great deal of hardship for me and both sides of our family. It has literally cost most of us our life's savings, and our middleclass lifestyle. The feeling is mutual amongst co-workers and friends.

Find out if your state is a "right to work" state. If it is, there is a good chance it is a non-union state. Take some time for you, and your children's future, and write a short letter to your state's governor or senator, protesting the pro-corporate/anti-worker policies in your state. A simple hand written letter will do. You don't have to be a professional writer, using big fancy words. All you will need is a piece of paper, an envelope, and a 32¢ stamp. You can get the address by calling your local Postal office, or calling any state agency listed in the yellow pages. It's very important to get the letters out! It's not quality but quantity of messages mailed. <u>Very important!!</u> When writing these officials about any problems whatsoever, use names of corporations, addresses, phone numbers, and people to contact. Again, I have to stress <u>Unity!</u> <u>Unity!</u> <u>Unity!!!</u> Also It's very important to be courteous and civilized. If there are several other people in the same predicament, join forces and complain jointly. When writing a joint letter, make sure all personal information such as names and addresses of each person involved, no matter how many. Make sure each individual signs his name at the bottom of the letter. Sample in the back of this book. This enables the readers to realize the broad scale impact the particular problem at hand is having on the lives of the citizens and their families. This definitely draws much more attention than a single gripe.

In the nation's larger cities, some of the more prominent television news media groups, news papers, have programs that sniff out raw deals dealt to citizens, employees and consumers by corporations, corrupt political leaders, and police enforcement. These undercover investigations tackle problems from substandard faulty merchandise, fraudulent repairs and services, to unsafe and unfair discriminatory employment practices. They won't be afraid to handle mass political and law enforcement corruption. In Miami/Ft. Lauderdale WSVN Channel 7 News offers a program called "The Real Deal" narrated by Carmel Cafiero. They have done wonders at public embarrassment, finger pointing, and uncovering some of the crapp dished out to the public by corporations and corrupt public officials. Crapp is king!!! There are also some national versions of such programs like 60 Minutes, Inside Edition, Hard Copy, ABCNews, and Dateline. I have used them more than once, to blow the whistle on bad merchandise, fraudulent services to unsafe, unfair employment practices. Sometimes just the mentioning of such a program at the right instance, when you feel you are getting the shaft, will nip the problem at the bud. Nothing on this planet is a better corporate attitude adjuster than these two words, BAD PRESS!

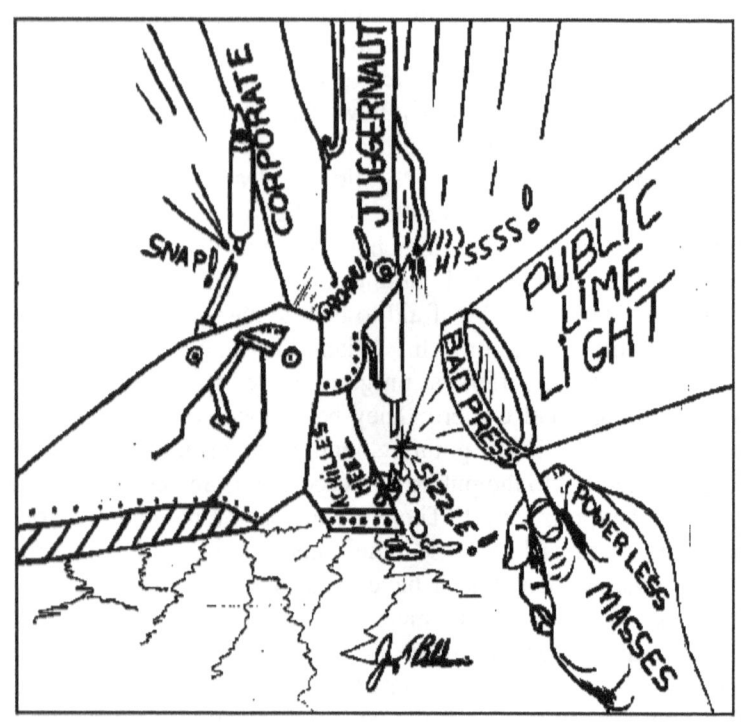

THE CHINK IN THE ARMOR "After more than a decade of corporate anarchy, the average person single handed is no match to the inexhaustible financial brawn and cunning legal prowess of a super corporation. However, these super giants have a common weakness BAD PRESS. With all their might, yet, like creatures of the night, they tremble helplessly, scurrying like rats in the face of negative publicity.. Every single man and woman in this country regardless of financial and social status, can bring these supposedly invincible juggernauts crashing to the ground. Unite with fellow employees and consumers, put your mind to it with determination by using your resources, but most of all, TRASH THEIR IMAGE.

[Illustration 31]

116

Support these media programs by using them whenever you feel your civil, employee, and consumer rights have been violated. Call your nearest big city's TV news station to get further details on such programs. These programs work only if a large number of complaints on a particular subject come in. They can conceal your identity, if you request it, as to protect your career, or to prevent any retaliation. It's your-responsibility as an American citizen to take some time cut of your busy schedule to unite with your co-workers and fellow consumers. This will send a sharp and concise message to corporate America, and the authorities "we aren't going to take it any more!" Go ahead, make their day, pick up that phone!

If you have problems with paychecks vs the hours call the Dept. of labor.

If you feel you have been sexually, racially, physically (because of a handicap), or religiously discriminated by an employer, you should notify your local Equal Employment Opportunity Board EEOC.

If you and your co-workers are forced to work in un-safe conditions, you should contact the local Occupational Health and Safety Administration OSHA.

If you have purchased a faulty product/service, and you can't get the problem worked out with the store's personnel, notify Consumer Affairs division.

If you have purchased a house, building or construction not meeting safety specifications, not what was advertised etc., call the local building code authority.

If you are forced to operate company equipment in an un-safe condition, contact the Department Transportation DOT for land operated vehicles, the Federal Aviation Administration FAA, or the National Transportation Safety Board NTSB for airborne equipment, the U.S. Coast Guard for sea faring equipment.

If you have been the victim of law enforcement abuse, call the local police internal affairs office.

If you know of massive political corruption, contact the state governor, and the state senator in Washington D.C.

If these smaller steps fail and you feel you are not getting a fair review from these policing agencies, do like I did with my wife's case, just keep going up the ladder until you reach the President. We must make it as hard as possible for the corporate crimes to go un- contested. This will reverse the tide into the favor of the American worker, and the American consumer. This is just a list of some of the actions you can take, if you don' t have any money to spare on legal fees. It will only cost you envelopes, stamps, phone calls, and E-mail if you desire. There surely are other methods at your disposal, use as many as possible at the same time if you can. We must take this serious matter into our own hands. However, we must do it in a non-destructive manner.

In the past few years, we have seen a sharp nationwide increase in work place violence. Work place violence has recently been more directed toward supervisors, ceos, and their families by dis-gruntled employees. Unfortunately, innocent by standers often become the victims as well. According to psychology specialists, the cause of the violence is a direct result of the new cut throat attitude on behalf of the employers. In the past the, work place was a more supportive, hospitable, and personable social environment. To our dismay, today it's cold, deceptive, and non-caring, yet the employer demands more production, loyalty, and respect for less pay. A new term was invented to label this new crisis in American society. The term "going postal" is used to describe any employee whom has gone over the edge, and committed work place violence. This term originated due to the first few notable cases were reported at U.S. Post offices. Psychological authorities say this trend will continue to increase as employers become more impersonal and indifferent toward their employees. This is just another sign of the times, proving a desperate need for change. People and social skills are now being offered for ceo's and managerial personal to try to prevent these problems. However, they stress, the only way to prevent these problems, is for employers to change their attitudes toward their workers. I am against these violent ends to a problem, because the workers will not gain any sympathy from society. It undermines any attempts to change the problem, and society feels more sympathy toward the corporate leaders. It would be more advantageous for the disgruntled workers to band together in unity, and utilize some of the more constructive methods in this book.

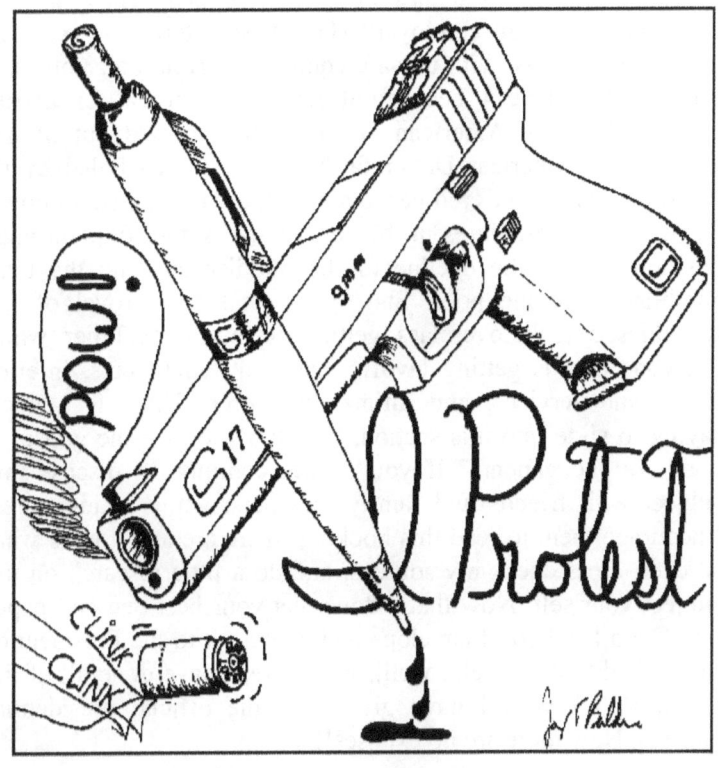

"BALLPOINTS ARE BETTER THAN BULLETS" Society is more sympathetic to angry pens than angry guns. "INK EM, DON'T ICE EM!"

[Illustration 32]

The next responsibility is probably the most important of all, if you really see the American middleclass lifestyle in danger. Take a pen, a piece of paper, and-a few minutes with family or friends to ask your self some serious questions from the heart. Am I better off financially now, than I was in the past? Am I living the quality of life for myself and/or for my family? Am I working longer, and harder for the same or less money, than in the past? Has my standard of living dropped? Have I been discriminated by an employer? Have I been forced to work in un-safe conditions, with un-safe equipment, even after notifying supervisors? Have I been fired for totally unfair, or untrue reasons? Has the American Dream been snatched out of my grasp? Is the American Dream farther out of my reach than ever?

If you have answered yes to any of these questions, jot down all of your dis-pleasures in the current status quo. Explain your position against the decline of the middleclass, and the total annihilation of the poor. State your total disapproval of the wealthiest 5%, the overclass, getting richer and wealthier, while everyone else is getting layoffs, pay and benefit cuts, inferior goods and services, and ultimately poorer. There is a good saying to slide into this section, "What's good for the goose, is good for the gander!" If you desire, continue to discuss this subject with friends and family members, while taking notes. Encourage them to read this book! If there are any doubts what so ever, cross check my sources, and do a little research on the subject your self. Now that's done, get your best pen and paper out. Get a legal sized envelope and address it to the President of the United States. Well.. well!, look here, I have done all of the leg work for you! I have given you the official presidential address. Now there are no excuses!!

President (full name here)

1600 Pennsylvania Ave.

Washington D.C. 20599-0001

Take the pen and paper and write a letter based on your notes and your conversation with families or friends. It doesn't have to be typed, just clearly written, straight to the point with no profanity. You don't have to use big fancy words, or legal jargon. Be business like, writing in your own words as if you were writing about a serious problem with a close business friend. Be courteous but firm, letting him know you are an unhappy camper. Here is my personal letter version written in one style of a common business format. For example:

(You're full name/address here)
1234 Lifestyle St.
Dreamville, Florida 33055
(101) 233-2000

(Date here)

(President's name/address here)
1600 Pennsylvania Ave.
Washington D.C. 20599-0001

Dear Mr. President:_____(name here)_____

I used to be a middleclass wage earner. As little as five to eight years ago, my family, friends, co-workers and I started to experience income stagnation/or substantial income decreases. Yet the cost of every day living continues to climb. Today, I am earning much less, however I am working twice as hard and putting in almost double the hours than I did in the past.

In a futile attempt to evade declining wages, learning skills in three different alternative trades, I now can no longer effectively support my family. Even with my wife working as well, our combined incomes do not equal the purchasing power of a single income a couple of decades ago.

After going bankrupt, loosing a nice home, all of our credit, a car, and our dignity, we are now at poverty level. The story is almost the same for other family members, friends, and co-workers. We are literally experiencing the "demise of the middleclass".

As this down ward mobile middleclass approaches the poverty line, ironically, we have witnessed an explosive increase in the personal incomes of the wealthy elite, ceo's and upper management of the nations larger corporations.

The American people, my family, and I formally protest this pillaging, and plundering of a people, a lifestyle, and a nation for the economic delight of the wealthy corporate overclass!! We will no longer tolerate this wealthiest 5% of the American population growing richer at our expense. I know you will realize the importance of returning the middleclass to the splendor and dignity it once had. Please address and consider a solution to this monumental crisis for the benefit for all of America. Thank You.

(Your signature here)

Leave the date and signature spaces blank on your original. Next make at least 12 copies of you're finished letter. Any office supply depot store has copy machines for the public's use at about 5 cents a copy. Now send one copy at the first of every month until the problem is addressed. The plan here is to nag him until something is done! I have learned in some of my cases the only way you get results and serious attention is to keep hammering away until something breaks. Do not always expect a response, as the president gets a lot of mail. Just because there is no response, doesn't mean he didn't receive it and hadn't read it.

If you absolutely can't send one out each month, choose one particular day of the year that is symbolic of the standard of living in America. April first is the last day to mail in income tax forms, represents the Standard of Living Improvement Day S.L.I.D, that all Americans can identify with. Don't be saying the American Dream SLID by you! The other reason I chose this particular day is the post office is experiencing one of the most busy days of the year outside of Christmas. The added mail burden will definitely gain some attention by government officials. There is one important warning!!!! <u>Do not send in the same envelope as you're income tax returns, or attached to it in any fashion!! The president will not get it, and you might delay you're income tax return!</u> Send separately!

We have to unite against this "in your face capitalist" beast devouring our very way of life. You are probably thinking how one little voice can be heard, unless you are rich and famous! A few hundred can cause a faint whisper. However, by the millions, we can cause an ear deafening roar! Through social conditioning and status quo, we have been "Brow Beaten", and "P _ _ _ y' whipped" to the point of submissiveness. The wealthy power elite prefer us this way! We offer no resistance, and no threat. The battle is won before it is ever started. It is, therefore, important to send out as many letters as possible. An important rule of thumb to follow, have everybody in each household, old enough to vote, send out a separate letter in his/her own wording. This is called voting without an official election day, and in the younger years of this country, these methods were surely used by early Americans, as well as scheduled voting days, to cast a ballot regarding an important subject. Let's show our founding fathers, we have not forgotten how to protest!! Like a single little red ant, you alone can leave an inconvenient sting behind. However, like the little red ants, by the millions, we Americans can bring down an elephant! Well here is your chance to make a difference! Our chance to get and take control of our destiny, our children's destiny, and to get up the destiny of the American way of life.

"United We Stand !" "Divided We Fall !" Many famous
people have spoken some version of these fateful words.
From the founding fathers of America, John F. Kennedy
quoting "Ask not what you're country can do for you, but
what you can do for you're country !", to Dr. Martin Luther
King and Nelson Mandella. Uniting with you're fellow
citizens is the ultimate power and right the people of a
democracy can exercise in conquering an overwhelming
common problem. It doesn't have to be an election year to
cast you're ballot addressing a problem. By the millions we
can persevere! Let's exercise our rights. Let's do something
for our country !!!!

[Illustration 33]

I am an ordinary blue collar worker, with a high school degree, no formal college education, no political affiliation, and no sociological background. All that I have learned I have learned through the University of Hard Knocks UHK. I have a Masters degree in daily life experiences down at the blue collar workers, life's eye view level. I honestly believe, by the experiences of my entire family, all of our friends, the people on the road, in the stores, on trains and planes, and our co-workers, we are witnessing an assault on our way of life more monumental than all of the wars in American history. I have an Associates degree in defiance, which has enabled me to take on the wealthiest and most powerful enemies with out so much as a flinch, even when all of the odds are against me. In the eyes of an enemy so well entrenched in American society, with so many more resources, my family and I, being one of a million to dare to defy status quo to bring change. Hence, we have suffered quit considerable. Being a pioneer is by no means a pleasurable adventure. It's a miserable job, but somebody has to do it!

If we can not out muscle them, we can give them a dose of their own medicine, making it harder for them to practice "in your face capitalism". Like a battered wife or an abused child, when they slap you around, get up in defiance, to spite the pain and suffering, and slap them back!!!!

Greed of one form or another has destroyed every civilization from the ancient Mesopotamians, the Greek Empire, the Roman Empire, all the way up to the German Empire known as the Third Reich. As with the barbarous leaders of these empires, today's corporate leaders are the Cleopatras, the Emperor Mings, the Julius Ceasars, and the Adolph Hitlers of tomorrow. These greedy corporate conquerors will be hell bent an exploiting people, and conquering societies to satisfy their "greed factor". The battle fields won't be open grassy meadows, but American society, and stock markets. Their weapons aren't going to be swords, guns, and tanks, but power, money, stocks, bonds, and worst of all, their largest and most powerful nuclear weapon will be "insatiable greed"! The innocent victims will not be shot, executed, and trampled under hoof or tread, but socio-economically devastated. Their lifestyles and standards of living will be stripped of all that's of value in the battle over financial resources, and financial power, like the countryside before an advancing hostile army. Like their barbaric counter parts, this corporate overclass will destroy society and our modern civilization in a financial apocalypse. Only the strongest leaders of the most powerful corporations will survive, and rule like emperors of a new scary world order. Therefore, it's the responsibility of every civilized individual to halt, and civilize these corporate barbarians if this civilization, as a whole, is to survive and flourish.

I have done my share by writing this book. I have spent hundreds of hours researching, and thousands of hours writing to create this message to the American middleclass working people. One percent inspiration, ninety nine percent perspiration! I have made the ultimate sacrifice in family time, my child, and my wife. My child has come up to me many times in my study asking for me to play with her, only for me to turn her away with tears in her eyes. Maybe one day she will realize, as I had with my father, I too, had a quest that I was determined to undertake, and then she will forgive me! I have not only made these sacrifices for my family and I, but for you and your families.

No doubt by writing this book, I have infuriated a lot of very wealthy elite people, in very high, powerful socio-economic positions. As my reader, if you happen to be a member of this greedy, wealthy elite, and I have insulted you, so be it!!!! According to the evidence at hand, not all of the socio-economic problems in America are a result of your so called "greed factor", but the lion's share of the smoking guns are in your hands! You can lay claim to one of the main reasons the middleclass and the poverty class are getting poorer. Most of the fingers are pointing in your direction. If the economy is really so bad as you make it out to be, then answer this question, why do you continue to give yourself and your upper management pay and benefit raises at the expense of the rest of your loyal workers? Why must you continue to rob from the working man, and the consumer, so you can pay yourself more? Well I've got news for you, most of the people out in the middleclass neighborhoods down to the ghettos, from all races and national origins share the same sentiments as I do! "What's good for the goose is good for the gander!" Keep those words in mind the next time you decide to give your employees pay and benefit cuts, or make them work in un-safe conditions so you can give yourself a juicy pay raise! You reap what you sow, and you haven' t been sowing much lately!

"THE END RESULT " You reap what you sow, and you
haven't been sowing much!

[Illustration 34]

One day it will catch up with you, don't worry!

If this book is successful in helping change the tides in the favor of the common working American, then I may be destined to the halls of martyrdom. This could very well result in the safety of my family and I being questionable. "You can kill the messenger, but you can't kill the message!" Wake up and smell the coffee, the message is out!

I have, by no means, forgotten those of you from this wealthy corporate elite, who honestly have good morals, choosing to sacrifice some of your own wealth potential so your employees can live much better! You are obviously more 'intelligent than some of your greedy counter parts, and realize the greater good to all, and American spirit. Some of you have gone as far as offering better paying jobs, with more benefits. Some of you have even gone as far as offering on site day care services to your family orientated employees. A happier, less concerned employee is a more loyal and productive worker. That's not the only way they will repay you. If they are earning more, they will have more money to spend on your goods and services, therefore stimulating the economy. Guess what? Every body is happier! Like a farmer sowing a crop, you will guarantee your own riches and wealth indefinitely. It's leaders with your foresight who had created a prosperous America in the past. Just maybe you can set an example for your more selfish, greedy peers! We, the American people, take our hats off to you. You have 100% of our support. Keep up the exceptional work, and thank you for attempting to raise the standard of living for all.

Well for you selfish, greedy sharks, the message is out. It's time to pay the piper. The free ride is over. The American masses will not tolerate the largest and most powerful corporate leaders to exploit entire nations, continents, and ultimately the entire planet with their global corporate empires. The world of tomorrow will not be ruled by these super wealthy corporate emperors, resulting in a nightmarish, Orwellian new world order. We will not allow the masses, middleclass and poverty class to be combined to form a new socio-economic class known as the Proletarian Class. The working middleclass, combined with the poor, out number you twenty to one. We won't be intimidated anymore. For the sake of this wonderful democracy, we will not allow America to be a haven for wealthy corporate leaders to make $millions not returning much to the faithful people who earned them these fortunes. We hold the future of this great land in our hands now, and we are not going away!!

Good luck fellow Americans! Spread the word, the pen is mightier than the sword. United you will make a difference now. Get those letters in the mail by the millions! Thank you for the interest in our future!

Psychologist Erich Fromm quoted:

"The history of man is a graveyard of great cultures that came to catastrophic ends because of their incapacity for planned, rational, voluntary reaction to challenge."

The Presidential mail drop! Consolidation in mass is the only way we can change the seemingly unchangeable status quo. <u>GET THOSE LETTERS IN THE MAIL</u>!

[Illustration 35]

END NOTES

This book is intended to be used as a middleclass workers hand book, and a practical informative moral booster. It attempts to draw the American public's attention to a serious social problem, and to alert them to the results of mass public complacency, and lack of concern over a long period of time resulting in negative social conditioning. It also uses practical hands on experience to re-build the American working public's self assertion, and esteem. It addresses ways to shatter years of social conditioning, status quo, and to re-educate the public on inexpensive, effective methods to counter corporate crimes, arrogance, greed, bias, and discrimination. To remind American citizens on their inherited powers and rights, to defy and change a flawed system that caters to the wealthy elite at the expense of the masses. Basically to give it's readers the practical tools to gallantly change the seemingly un-changeable, and to stamp out all feelings of hopelessness to regain access to the American Dream for the majority, not the wealthiest few.

The primary goal of this book is to warn the American working masses to the real possibility of the middleclass slipping downward and merging with the poverty class. This could result in the formation of a plutocratic society, in which the corporate emperors, their families (the wealthiest 5% population) and their mega corporate empires will socio-economically rule, dominate, and exploit the remaining 95% of the American people. If the American citizens do not unite, as they have never done before, the future will be a hopeless, bleak , empty, day to day struggle to survive for the majority of the American citizens. Also to stress that the current status quo isn't going to go away by ignoring it.

If there is any doubt in the minds of my readers, I strongly urge them to cross check my sources, perform an information search in various sociological references, search articles on middleclass economic trends, and perform interviews of average every day working middleclass citizens.

Asking them questions on work experiences, personal economic trends and security in the past, present, and future.

But most of all to look at their own economic journey, and quality of living trends. Thanks for taking an interest in you're future, you're children's future, and the future of America.

Other mandatory readings for all Americans and their families!

America: Who Stole The Dream? by Donald L. Barlett and James B. Steele.

America: What Went Wrong? by Donald L. Barlett and James B. Steele.

The End of Sanity! Social and Cultural Madness in Americas by Martin L. Gzoss.

The State of Americans by Urie Bronfenbrenner, Peter McClelland, Elaine Wethington, Phyllis Moen, and Stephen J. Ceci.

Who Will Tell The People? by William Greider.

IMPORTANT THINGS TO KNOW

Here is an important list of Federal, State, local agencies and public news media sources, that can come in real handy. The state agency phone numbers listed here are only for Florida. Each state has it's regional version of each of these offices. The phone numbers are available by dialing information. I have used a good portion of them for some of my cases. Don't let them get away with it!!! Bad press, and negative publicity is the most powerful corporate attitude adjuster on the planet!

AGRICULTURE & CONSUMER SERVICES DEPT. OF

Regional for each state. 1-800-453-7352(Florida only)

BUSINESS & PROFESSIONAL REGULATION DEPT. OF

Regional for each state. 1-800-432-79400(Florida only)

CONSUMER AFFAIRS

Regional for each county.

ENVIRONMENTAL PROTECTION DEPT. OF

Regional for each state. (407)   433-2650(S. Florida only)

EQUAL EMPLOYMENT OPPORTUNITY COMMISSION E.E.O.C.

Regional for each major city,

GOVERNOR STATE OF FLORIDA

(904) 488-7146 or 488-4441

HEALTH & REHABILITATIVE SERVICES DEPT. OF

Regional for each state. 1-800-962-2873(Florida only)

INSIDE EDITION TV   Whistle Blower Hotline 1-900-B-INSIDE toll call

LABOR DEPT.   Regional for each city.
   WAGE & HOUR

LABOR LAW ATTORNEYS   See Yellow Pages
   Specialized private attorneys that handle labor law disputes.

NATIONAL TRANSPORTATION
   & SAFETY BOARD   Regional for each city.
   N.T.S.B.

OCCUPATIONAL SAFETY
   & HEALTH   Regional for each major city.
   ADMINISTRATION O.S.H.A.

PRESIDENT OF THE UNITED STATES
1600 Pennsylvania Avenue
Washington D.C. 20599-001

TRANSPORTATION   Regional for each city.
   DEPT. OF D.O.T.

UNION AFL-CIO Free beneficial informative American worker update line. Regular free updates on bills, legislation, and laws that directly effect both non-union, and union American workers. 1-800-765-4440 <u>FREE!!!</u>

UNION, AMALGAMTED TRANSIT   Regional for each city.

UNION, TEAMSTERS   Regional for each city.

UNION, LONGSHOREMAN"S   Regional for port cities.

I have compiled a sample menu of some typical letters you might need for various situations. These are in business format, but are just for your reference as content will vary according to your own personal situation. Use them as structure samples to start your own letters.

Remember, if you send one to the President, also send one addressed to the governor of your state, or vise versa. Let each receiving party know that the other party also received a similar letter. This way if they contact each other on your matter, they will have similar copies. Reason number two, and most importantly, <u>psychology!!</u> This sends a concise message, that you mean business, and there is definitely a problem.

Remember, extreme patience and diligent persistence are the most vital ingredient, and may seem futile and a waist of time at the moment, but later on will pay off. Don't give in to corporate arrogance, and disrespect' "United we stand!" "Divided we fall!"

Sample A
(Individual correspondence)

(Your name, and address here)
1234 Lifestyle Street
Banksville, Florida 33056

(The date here)

President <u>(name here)</u>
1600 Pennsylvania Ave.
Washington D.C. 20599-001

Dear Mr. President,

I was a sales associate at Thingamajig Corporation 1201 Profit St. Miami, Florida 33011-011 phone {954) 233-2000 I was terminated from my job last week because of my child's on-going sickness, which required regular scheduled visits to the hospital. My supervisor Mr. John B. Rich was perfectly aware of the days and hours I needed. He told me I was no longer allowed to have time off from work for any reason. He commented that I had to make a choice between family or career. He added, if I left to take my child to the hospital, he would have to do what he has to.

I feel I was terminated for unjust reasons, and out right lies. My termination papers stated reasons for termination was lack of performance and improper attitude.

I have filled a legal suit for $80,000 in damages with the Department of Labor's Equal Employment Opportunity Commission, but I feel they aren't enough to stop this unfair and unjust treatment to the working parents of America. Copies of the complaint and legal proceedings to date are enclosed. I have no money to hire expensive attorneys, there fore, I am depending on the Federal agencies to get the justice, I deserve.

I hope you realize the importance of changing the system to benefit the working parents instead of the wealthy corporate leaders, and prevent future parents from going through similar situations. Thank you very much!

(Your signature here)
(Print your name here)

Sample B
(Multiple person correspondence)

(Each person's name and address here)
Jack Doe
1234 Lifestyle Street
Banksville, Georgia 33011

John Doe
43210 Broke Street

Banksville, Georgia 3301

Jane Doe
120 Work Way Cobb, Georgia

Governor's (name here)
123 Peachtree St.
Atlanta, Georgia 33104

Dear Governor,

We are several employees with the Build Em Right Construction Corp. 700 Roof Truss Way Banksville, Georgia 33021 (770) 321-9900.

We have reported ongoing safety hazards and un-safe run down equipment to our supervisor Mr. Jack B. Good. After two or more weeks of no positive response, we mentioned it to manager Sam B. Badd. After a lot of reassurances, it has been several months, and nothing has been done. Some of us have refused to operate the un-safe equipment, and have faced ridicule and disciplinary actions from the management for insubordination. One employee was fired for this, however his termination papers stated he was fired for failure to operate company equipment in a safe manner.

After this action, and the appearance nothing is ever going to be done, we filled a complaint with the Occupational Safety and Health Administration (O.S.H.A.). We feel injunction with the complaint to O.S.H.A., you should be aware of the lack of concern and unfair treatment on the corporation's part. We have sent a similar letter to the President of the United States. We have enclosed copies of the complaint filled with O.S.H.A., and any correspondence up to date. We wish to remain anonymous to the company to protect our careers. We need to have these concerns addressed as soon as possible for the safety of the workers and the public. We hope you will realize the true dangers to the employee work force, and the general public assisting us in any way you can. Thank you very much!

(All signatures here)
(Print all names under signatures)

Example of extended more personal in detail version.

John Doe
2020 Pine Dr.
Plantation, Florida. 33315

The President of the United States
1600 Pennsylvania Avenue
Washington D.C. 20599-001

Dear Mr. President,

My wife and I are hard working middle-class Americans. We used to live comfortably the American Dream with a middle-class lifestyle. Every thing we had we earned through hard work and loyalty in the work place. However, the last 5-7 years our economic status has slipped into the poverty zone. We are now the working poor. Today we can barely put food on the table, much less live the quality of life we were used to.

My wife was terminated from her good paying job in early 1994. This was because she needed to take our seriously ill daughter for regular visits to the doctors, and to the Hospital twice a month, for a total of 6 hours per visit, for monitoring purposes and medication purposes. Her supervisor gave her the ultimatum to make a choice between family and career one day when she reminded the supervisor of an up coming scheduled visit to the doctors. My wife did what any mother would do, she took the child to the doctors. She was terminated shortly after.

After fumbling around with private attorneys, the labor board, and finally the Equal Employment Opportunity Commission (E.E.0.C.). we opened a case against the corporation for violation of state and federal Family Leave Acts. This has been a 5 year, all up hill, battle! The E.E.0.C. had been less than cooperative, and tried to drop the case at least once.

It's your word against theirs, they kept saying, even though we had two witnesses. We were constantly reminded Florida is a right to work state, and labor laws have less power. I vowed to some way have recording devices on both of us every day at work. In the future they will have their evidence!! We appealed the decision of the E.E.O.C. to side with the corporation. We also sent letters of protest to Governor Lawton Chiles, Connie Mack in the senate, and first lady Hillary Clinton protesting the lack of concern, and in-efficiency of the E.E.0.C. We also protested the fact the system, rules, and laws are basically designed to protect corporations and their leaders at the expense of the little guy.

Amidst record corporate profits, and skyrocketing executive and CEO income, my income has slowly dropped from around $11 an hour in the 1980s, to around $8-$9 an hour today, with less benefits, in the same fields of my experience. We are working much harder and putting in longer hours at the work place, yet the cost of every day living keeps creeping upward.

I, other members of our family, and our peers have been terminated for various reasons. My mother was terminated from her lifetime career with a Dept. store corporation in the 1980s 2 years before retirement with full pension. This was because in her aging condition she needed to visit the ladies room more than the company would allow. When we fought it, they had other reasons, such as poor performance, etc. A typical tactic practiced by all corporations when one is fired for other reasons.

I have been terminated from various careers for refusing to operate unsafe equipment, or reprimanded for insubordination

141

for not complying with company orders even if it meant potential harm to the public, myself, or the environment. I have been terminated for totally ridiculous reason such as stopping my truck to use the restroom, or taking a non-paid lunch hour. The orders were made clear not to stop for any reason whatsoever, if you really needed lunch, you take your lunch from home and eat it while driving. Yet the company deducted an hour out of your pay daily for lunch!!

My life was made impossible at work, when I challenged them, after calling the labor board and finding out driving time does not dictate un-paid lunch time, refused, or made a big deal about being forced to operate unsafe equipment. I would always get fired shortly after, for totally un-true reasons, insubordination, poor performance, or some other lie.

This would result in a catch twenty two situation. In some instances my co-workers as well as I would elect to comply with company orders and operate the equipment. Some instances did result in an accident, and we, the employees, would be reprimanded and written up for un-safe operation of company equipment. If we chose to remind management of our previous reports of the un-safe situation, our intelligence would then be insulted, by being told if the operation was done safely regardless of the defect, the accident would not have occurred. It was apparent if one showed any sense of virtue, or an intelligent head on our shoulders, we were basically singled out and eventually terminated. The trick to keep your job was to blindly follow all directives, asking no questions whatsoever, and take your discipline un-disputed, even though you were used as a scape goat.

In 1995 I worked with a pest control company. Six months into what appeared to be a great career, They decided to re-organize to cut back on expenses. This meant more time and responsibilities on our part, at nights, at home and on weekends. Overtime compensation on the responsibilities performed at home was stopped. This meant almost a 50% pay cut for all of us! Other un-ethical activities were used to keep expenses down. Improper storage of pesticides, cheaper less effective materials were used in customer's homes, mixing dosages were diluted to half to one third of the labels directions, solutions not labeled for certain uses were implemented when stocks were depleted, trucks and equipment became un-safe and neglected resulting in serious chemical spills, etc. To rub salt into the wound, our bonuses for cross marketing leads slowed to a trickle. Some of us began a campaign of keeping track of sales and found out a good percentage of closed sales were not on our bonus lists. We would inquire about these discrepancies with our lead numbers to company headquarters in Atlanta as we were instructed to do. Atlanta would claim the leads never sold and could not compensate us for the sales. I even made calls from several customer's homes so as to have un-disputable proof with receipts, etc.

I would be lectured again in some instances by a supervisor no sale was reported and no bonuses would be issued. Those of us, me included, who made a big deal out of this ended up with a sudden flood of customer complaints supposedly made on the 800 line to Atlanta. We were then terminated immediately, for poor performance, by memo directly from Atlanta.

There are other methods, I have witnessed or experienced first hand, that corporate America employs to lower expenses and ultimately raise profit margins along with executive salaries. All done at the customer's and working man's expense!

More corporations today tend to hire from temporary services instead of full time company employees. I suppose to avoid paying benefits, holidays, vacations, etc.

Corporations are hiring more part time employees, sometimes multiple shifts per day, to make a full day of work. They do not have to pay any benefits, holidays, retirements, paid vacations, etc.

Another popular method companies utilize to avoid paying benefits, holiday, vacations, retirement, etc., really strikes hard at lower income workers requiring little or no training. They hire employees at sub standard wages, then terminate them before their 90th probationary day. This cycle is then repeated indefinitely in areas of high transient, International, and large populations. I have been a victim of this one as well. These firms literally run ads in the classified sections 52 weeks of the year! The great revolving door. Next victim please!!

Social conditioning is seen at it's worst in this most popular method of all. As job openings occur either through some of the methods mentioned above, or through attrition, the replacement workers would be hired at a starting wage below that of previous starting wages. Doing this gradually over a period of time, the masses are being socially conditioned to accept a lower income standard and a lower quality of life than in past years.

January 6, 1998 I was terminated from another pest control job. I was not given any reason other than we don't need your services any longer. This was shortly after my supervisor hired a replacement worker to train before Christmas 97. I however Know the real reason I was terminated. December 1, 1997 I refused to remove my shoes in a customer's home during a pesticide application. I have 9 years in the pest control industry, and know not to apply pesticides without leather shoes, and long pants. My supervisor lectured me rather arrogantly in front of two other employees. He said, in a nut shell, I would remove my shoes if the customer requests, and it is the policy of the company. If I don't remove my shoes, I would be looking for a job somewhere else. I still refused, and he told me he would take me out there to the customer's home and make me take my shoes off and service the home. I refused this venture! Because of the variety of experiences our family as well as my personal dealings with corporate arrogance, I now carry a small microcassette recorder concealed on me at all tines while at work. I got the entire lecture on tape. I have been told time and again, It's my word against theirs, and my word is basically not worth much

144

against a corporations. Well now with a clear and precise recording, holding them to their words forever, for all to hear, they can not change their version! End of all questions!!!! Since that day the owner of the company as well as the supervisor, even though they knew nothing of the recorded lecture, seemed to take on a different attitude toward me!

After this, I started to call local state and federal departments, such as the Occupational Safety and Health Administration (O.S.H.A.), the Dept. of Agriculture, and the Bureau of Entomology. Persistence and patience seemed to be the tune fore the day. Wild goose chases, phone tag, un-preparedness, un-returned messages, lack of concern, under staffed and under financed offices seem to be common among all of these departments. I spent dozens of hours haggling with these departments for my wife's case five years ago, as well as some of my other cases. The system designed to protect employees and consumers is archaic, inefficient, and un-sensitive to the needs of the clients. For simple minded blue collar workers, with no experience in these matters, this can be an un-imaginable, overwhelming navigational nightmare. My family and I have probably used this system more than most people in this country, and we still feel as though we have left the beaten path, with macheties in hand, into an un-charted jungle. If there is going to be any justice for the little guy, this system must be made more user friendly!

I have done two and a half years of public interviews from all ages, races and career back grounds. Over 8 out of every 10 people support these accusations, and identify a serious social problem in the United States. However, 7 of those 8 people, who have identified this problem, and agree with me, will never even try to change the status quo or even seek justice for themselves or their families. A common belief is; "It's too much of a hastle!" "It's a waste of time!" "I don't have the time!" "What's the use!" "Nothing will change!" "That's life!" "One little voice will not be heard!" "Unless you have money, nobody cares!" "You won't make a difference!" "No matter what you do nothing will change" "Justice is for the affluent!". The list goes on with a whole list of other tuck your tail between your legs sayings. This has really got me concerned. The masses have completely lost all faith in the system and America! Public attorneys are also out of range financially of the average working class citizen. The only ones that seem completely content in the current status quo are executives, business owners, those in power, and the affluent. I speak not only for myself in this letter, but for the working American people. This leaves little or no alternatives for the little guy. The system as a whole is more geared to protect corporate America, the wealthy, and those in power at the expense of the working Americans and consumers. With all of these factors, social conditioning and status quo on their side, corporations are raking in record profits, ceo's and executives are paying themselves record salaries and are laughing all the way to the bank. The rich are getting richer, the middleclass and poor are getting poorer! It appears corporate exploitation of a people, and a society is on a rapid increase and is totally out of control. The have have more now than at any other time in American history. It's at a 64 year high! Is this our destiny? Has the American Dream became only for the wealthiest few, and has become an American nightmare for the rest of us? Are we living in a socio-economic totalitarian state, if those with the money and power are the only ones capable of changing the system, refuse to change it for fear of loosing some of their financial influence, and power? Must the consequences of domestic affairs be shouldered by those least able to shoulder them. The founding fathers must be doing somersaults in their graves, and did not intend for the system to be used this way!

I realize a lot has been done to help the little guy, the Family leave Act, small Tax cuts for working parents, a raise in the minimum wage, etc., but these are drops in the barrel. Even un-employment is at an all time low, but all of these new jobs are in much lower income fields, and the people working them are accustomed to much larger salaries all of their lives as in past years. A whole new code of ethics must be adopted by corporate America instead of an insatiable greed factor and the bottom line. This must be addressed if this civilization is going survive and prosper. Capitalism used to be our friend, however now, that can be questionable. Maybe a more utilitarian style capitalism should be the driving force of our nation's economy benefiting the working masses, instead of just the wallets of the wealthiest few.

There has been a sudden explosion of new books in the social sciences sections of the nations book stores in the past few years addressing these very problems. My book, "Delight of The Overclass, Demise of the Middleclass", will also some day, be available to the public alerting them, and educating them of various ways to combat corporate exploitation, arrogance, social conditioning, and status quo. It urges every single American to take a more aggressive posture in politics by speaking up, and by voting not just on election days but any time a problem arises The percentages of voter turn out is utterly pathetic now days. It also counters the utterly helpless feeling most Americans feel in countering negative social conditioning. The people must no longer be silent, hen pecked passive sheep being led around by the rings in their noses, the sleeping giant is slowly awakening, and is filled with a terrible resolve!

If you are a man of virtue, with any code of ethics, you will realize the American people must not allow the American Dream to slip into the hands of the wealthiest few, living an increasingly gluttonous and greedy lifestyle. We will not allow the middle-class and the poor to continue to slip into lower standards of living, ironically while working harder and longer hours at the work place with less and less reward.

Our children must not inherit a proletarian two class society, with the richest 5% exploiting socially and financially the remaining 95% of the population.

I have sent similar copies of this letter to the Governor of Florida, Florida Senator Connie Mack, all of the senators of the remaining states, and the nation's most prominent Television investigative press agencies. Thank you for your time and concern for the future of this great nation. The concerned working little people whom make America possible!

Sincerely,

Example of a stern, forcefull, dictatorial version.

January 2, 1998

Regional Administrator
U.S. Dept. of Labor- OSHA/11c
Atlanta Federal Center
61 Forsyth St. SW
Atlanta, Georgia 30303

RE: Forced removal of shoes during a pesticide application/Baldwin/1116129

Dear Sirs,

It seems the word of a humble working blue collar worker is not trustworthy compared to a lying corporation. I and my family have utilized many federal government departments for various cases in the past from employment disputes, discrimination disputes, safety disputes, to consumer rights disputes. One constant that is familiar, and I have noticed that seems to be prevalent in all of our families cases, is the willingness of the system as a whole to unanimously always side with the corporation in question. No matter how hard we have tried we have never won a single case against a corporation. Is this my imagination, or is this the operative goals of all government Depts. ????

Must the decisions and consequences of all government Depts. be shouldered by those least able to shoulder them. Is this an Oligarchy or a democracy? What is the difference between

148

my word and their word? Does the fact that a corporation is a corporation automatically make it's word the wholeheartedly, unquestionably the truth beyond a reasonable doubt?

Well my friends me and my family have learned from our lessons. We no longer go to work, or anywhere our word might be questioned without a concealed audio recording device on our persons. Now we have the upper hand and the evidence is permanently recorded for the ears of the world and the press to hear. We are doing the last conceivable attempt to seek justice in a system with all of the odds stacked against us. We are starting a revolution of a sort. I am spreading my corporate anti-terrorist counter measures in a variety of ways to the oppressed working people of America. Giving them the ability to level the playing field.

Please listen to this copy of the tape I recorded a couple of weeks prior to my termination. This is the Vice President of my company telling me to take my shoes off while spraying or I will be working someplace else! Now compare that to your supposedly thorough investigation!!! Unfortunately, the working man in this situation was telling the truth after all and the supposedly trustworthy, reliable, innocent corporation was lying through their teeth! I suggest you completely re-evaluate your investigation procedures for the sake of the American people. We will no longer be swept under the carpet without a fight. I have multiple copies of this letter and the audio tape ready to roll over to WSVN Channel 7 News Carmel Cafiero's Real Deal, Inside Edition in New York, and a couple of investigative reporters at the Time Warner bldg. headquarters of Time magazine in New York. Justice is no longer just for the affluent. For the sake of all at hand please re-consider my appeal as nothing but the truth so help me God!!!!

Sincerely a seriously concerned struggling American worker,

Governor's addresses of 50 states in alphabetical order by State.

Alabama: Office of the Governor 600 Dexter Ave, Montgomery.

Alaska: Office of the governor P.O. Box 110001, Juneau.

Arizona: Office of the Governor 1700 West Washington St., Phoenix.

Arkansas: Office of the Governor State Capital Room 250, Little Rock.

California: Office of the Governor State Capitol 1st Floor, Sacramento.

Colorado: Office of the Governor State Capitol Bldg. Room 136, Denver.

Connecticut: Office of the Governor Executive Chambers 210 Capitol Ave., Hartford.

Delaware: Office of the Governor Tatnall Bldg., William Penn St., Dover.

Florida: Office of the Governor The Capitol, Tallahassee.

Georgia: Office of the Governor 203 State Capitol, Atlanta.

Hawaii: Office of the Governor State Capitol 415 S. Beratania Ave. Honolulu.

Idaho: Office of the Governor P.O. Box 83720, Boise.

Illinois: Office of the Governor Capitol Bldg. Room 207, Springfield.

Indiana: Office of the Governor State Capitol Room 206, Indianapolis.

Iowa: Office of the Governor State Capitol Bldg., Des Moines.

Kansas: Office of the Governor State Capitol 2nd Floor, Topeka.

Kentucky: Office of the Governor 700 Capitol Ave., Frankfort.

Louisiana: Office of the Governor P.O. Box 94004, Baton Rouge.

Maine: Office of the Governor 1 State House Station, Augusta.

Maryland: Office of the Governor State House, Annapolis.

Massachusetts: Office of the Governor Executive Office 360, Boston.

Michigan: Office of the Governor P.O. Box 30013, Lansing.

Minnesota: Office of the Governor State Capitol Room 130, St. Paul.

Mississippi: Office of the Governor P.O. Box 139, Jackson.

Missouri: Office of the Governor P.O. Box 720, Jefferson City.

Montana: Office of the Governor Capitol Bldg., Helena.

Nebraska: Office of the Governor P.O. Box 94848, Lincoln.

Nevada: Office of the Governor Capitol Complex, Carson City.

New Hampshire: Office of the Governor State House 107 N. Main Room 208, Concord.

New Jersey: Office of the Governor State House CN 001, Trenton.

New Mexico: Office of the Governor State Capitol Room 400, Santa Fe.

New York: Office of the Governor Executive Chambers State Capitol, Albany.

North Carolina: Office of the Governor 116 W. Jones St., Raleigh.

North Dakota: Office of the Governor 600 E. Boulevard Ave., Bismarck.

Ohio: Office of the Governor 77 S. High St. 30th Floor, Columbus.

Oklahoma: Office of the Governor State Capitol Room 212, Oklahoma City.

Oregon: Office of the Governor State Capitol Bldg. Room 254, Salem.

Pennsylvania: Office of the Governor Main Capitol Bldg. Room 225, Harrisburg.

Rhode Island: Office of the Governor 143 State House, Providence.

South Carolina: Office of the Governor P.O. Box 11369, Columbia.

South Dakota: Office of the Governor 500 E. Capitol Ave., Pierre.

Tennessee: Office of the Governor State Capitol Bldg., Nashville.

Texas: Office of the Governor P.O. Box 12428, Austin.

Utah: Office of the Governor 210 State Capitol, Salt Lake City.

Vermont: Office of the Governor Pavilion Office Bldg. 109 State. St., Montpelier.

Virginia: Office of the Governor State Capitol Bldg. 3rd Floor, Richmond.

Washington: Office of the Governor Legislative Bldg., Olympia.

West Virginia: Office of the Governor 1900 Kanawha Blvd. E. Capitol Bldg., Charleston.

Wisconsin: Office of the Governor P.O. Box 7863, Madison.

Wyoming: Office of the Governor State Capitol Bldg. 124 200 W. 24th St., Cheyenne.

BIBLIOGRAPHY

Adler, Jerry. "The Overclass" <u>Newsweek</u>, July 31, 1995, pp. 32-35.

Barlett, Donald L., Steele, James B. <u>America What Went Wrong?</u>. Missouri: Andrews and McMeel, 1992.

Bronfenbrenner, Urie., McClelland, Peter., Wethington, Elaine., Moen, Phyllis., Ceci, Stephen J. <u>The States of Americans</u>. New York: The Free Press, 1996.

Eitzen, D, Stanly., Zinn, Maxine Baca. <u>In Conflict and Order</u>. Needham Heights: Allyn and Bacon, 1995.

Fox, Justin. "Big Labor Flexes It's Muscles." <u>Fortune</u>. June 10,1996, pp. 24-26

Fong, Kathrine. "Readers see many causes for growing income gap" <u>The Herald </u>November 4, 1996, p. 5.

Greenfield, Jeff. "Voter anxiety: A Chronic Condition" <u>Time</u> April 22, 1996, p. 58.

<u>Handbook For Writers</u>. Englewood Cliffs: Prentice-Hall, Inc., 1985.

Lublin, Joann S. "Why More People Are Battling Over Bonuses" <u>The Wall Street Journal</u>. January 8, 1997, p. B1, p. B7.

Lublin, Joann S. "Don't Count On That Merit Raise This Year" <u>The Wall Street Journal</u>, January 7, 1997, p. B1, p. B6.

"Machinist's Strike Stalls Jetmaker." <u>USA Today</u> 6 June 1996, sec. B, p.3, col.2.

Perry, John., Perry Erna K. Contemporary Society. New York: Harper & Row Publishers, 1984.

Samuelson, Robert J. "The Politics Of Self-Pity." Newsweek, February 26, 1996, p. 50.

Schwartz, David J. The Magic Of Thinking Big. New York: Fireside Simon & Schuster, 1987.

Shellenbarger, Sue. "Family Leave Is Law, But Climate Is Poor For Actually Taking It" The Wall Street Journal, October 30, 1996, p. Bl.

Sloan, Allan. "The Hit Men." Newsweek, February 26, 1996, pp. 44-48.

Smolowe, Jill. "The Stalled Revolution." Time, May 6, 1996, pp. 44-48.

Smolowe, Jill. "Reap As Ye Shall Sow." Time, February 5, 1996, p. 63.

Thomas, Rich. "A Rising Tide Lifts The Yachts." Newsweek, May 1, 1995, p. 62D.

Quinn, Jane Bryant. "A Paycheck Revolt In '96 ?" Time, February 19, 1996, p. 52.

Williams Gordon, "The Wealth And Health Of Our Nation" The American Legion, October 1996, pp. 20-21, p. 51.

A.P.A.D.D.

Americans to Preserve the American Dream and Democracy

America the land of the free and the home of the American dream. A democratic wonderland where the masses enjoy freedom of choice and are catered to by a civil service government loyal only to the people. A socio-economic paradise based on a capitalist free market economy which, in the past, gave rise to the largest and strongest middleclass, living comfortably the American dream, in human history. Well my fellow Americans better think again! This is the way it used to be! However, today amidst a roaring economy for the corporate elite, booming Wallstreet figures, record corporate profits and greed of historical proportions, the American middleclass family, barely able to make ends meet with two full time incomes, under the spell of social conditioning, is slowly being dismantled into a proletarian worker servant class. To rub salt into the wound, a record number of freedoms and privileges are being altered, neutralized or purged from our constitution and law books while American freedoms of choice are slowly being revoked with authoritarian oppression by the vary elected individuals installed to protect them. Our country is beginning to resemble the worlds largest autocratic oligarchy, or a kinder gentler totalitarian police state. America is a plutocracy.

157

Yes! A plutocracy where a band of wealthy powerful corporate and political elite, in high places, create legislation, rules and regulations that benefit mainly this elite, all the while they dominate, manipulate, economically and socially the American masses, greedily exploiting them for their labor, resources and political votes.

Yes! A police state which continually but slowly attempts to erase freedom of choice, liberties and American rights and a strong independent middleclass using social conditioning over a long period of time. Today, a man's home or castle is no longer his to do with as he likes. Some counties, cities and communities dictate what color to paint your home, what kind and how many cars you can drive, what kind and how much landscaping you can plant, what kind, how much and where to enjoy recreation, how many children, if any, you can have. If you do not believe me, a typical day at any south Florida beach speaks a thousand words. In the 60's, 70's and early 80's a typical Sunday afternoon at any south Florida beach showed a myriad of recreation activities from windsurfers, small sail boats, catamarans, jetskis, scuba divers, snorkelers, paddleballs, frisbees, kites, model boats and a whole host of free and happy people frolicking in the waves. Today, like some transformation into a George Orwell science fiction novel after decades of authoritarian oppression, new regulations and state, county and city ordinances a day at the beach consists of masses of poker faced bathers, umbrellas, towels and sun tan lotion bottles glistening in the sun, while dozens of multimillion dollar yachts sail slowly by. Most beach front counties and cities now limit the number and class of people privileged to have access to any beach property by limiting parking with less spaces or charging outlandish fees. Some no longer allow access unless you belong to a certain economic class who can afford waterfront property. Now you have millions of landlocked people. It seems only a wealthy privileged few can reap freedom of choice anymore. Ask anybody what happened to the middleclass recreational American dream pie and you will get the same answers. Too many rules, regulations and laws so all we do now is take a towel and sun screen and watch the yachts go by. Just take a look at the signs on most American beaches; No boat launching!, No scuba diving or snorkeling!, No surfing!, No picnics!, No food or drinks!, No balls!, No frisbees!, No kites!, No innertubes!, No playing!, No fun!!, No smiling!!!, No anything!!! I thought this was America? Seems more like the late Soviet Union.

Are you tired of politics as usual? Are you sick of an irresponsible dysfunctional government? Do you feel the government has forgotten who it works for? Do you feel we are now the servants of the government? Do you feel the government is laced with greedy, corrupted political leaders? Do you feel our government has become too intrusive into the lives of the average citizen but does not exercise enough control over it's self or wealthy powerful corporations and their elite leaders? Do you feel the constitution laid out by our founding fathers is slowly and inconspicuously being dismantled? Do you feel our society is full of greed, bias and double standards? Do you feel freedom of choice is being slowly narrowed with each passing day? Do you feel the government is too apathetic in dealing with the needs and desires of the middleclass average citizen? Do you feel the middleclass, as we once knew it, will be gone in the not too distant future? Do you feel the middleclass is no longer living the standard of living or quality of life it used to? Do you feel the wealthy elite and corporate leaders, a scant 5% of the population will continue to reap record profits and incomes while most families, now even with two incomes, can no longer make ends meet? Do you feel our society will soon become a caste based society with a dominating overclass while everyone else struggles by as the proletariat working class? Do you feel most labor law violations, against working Americans, by wealthy powerful corporations go unpunished? Do you feel most consumer law violations by wealthy, influential corporations against the American consumer go unpunished? Do you feel American justice has become contorted, twisted, and distorted and is no longer effective? Do you feel criminals have more rights than the victims? Do you feel most laws apply only to the masses and not to wealthy, famous or influential individuals, the government and mega corporations? Has our country become the laughing stock of the world in the face of rampant scandal, political corruption across the board including capital hill? Are you ashamed to be an American? Is this the America our founding fathers and our brave service men have fought and died for? Is this the America you want your children growing up in? Must rights, liberties, privileges and freedom of choice be reserved for the highest bidders? Is America for sale to only those who can afford it?

If you said no to the last four and yes to the rest, join a shocking 80% of the middleclass and poor who share the same view point, now it is time to become a self declared member of A.P.A.D.D, We can no longer afford to have an apathetic, that's life, there is nothing we can do, or some other tuck your tail between your legs and give up attitude. If we refuse to do something now, we may witness the delight of the overclass and the demise of the middleclass ending in an apocalyptic class war where nobody will win. Are you willing to take that chance with our future? (See graph courtesy of the Internal Revenue service on last page of introduction.)

There are no out of pocket expenses, dues or fees to join A.P.A.D.D. or any other requirements other than being a citizen of the United States registered to vote, and have an overwhelming desire for a more free, prosperous, and democratic America. You also must also be willing to bravely stand up for what you believe in!

The A.P.A.D.D. United Declaration of Virtues on the preceding pages does not have a copy right and is there fore you to make copies of. Please be free to make as many copies as you can! Hand them out to your friends and family members who may not have printers or computers. Next sign and date inserting your address, place in an envelope addressed to the President of the United States and mail at once.

President_____of the United States of America
1600 Pennsylvania Avenue
Washington D.C. 20599-001

Next mail a copy to your senator, congressman, all the way down to your local elected officials.

Consider this a formal warning from the American people united!

"United we stand, divided we fall!"
Pad the American Dream and Democracy with A.P.A.D.D.

Concerned citizen
President and founder of A.P.A.D.D.
Jay T. Baldwin

A.P.A.D.D.

Americans to Preserve the American Dream and Democracy

United Declaration of Virtues

We the people of the United States of America, in order to restore a more perfect union, have united as Americans to preserve the American dream and democracy and as a people united of all races, religions and national origins in an American democracy as a majority, will no longer tolerate the following unethical, undemocratic and unconstitutional, plutocratic, autocratic activities in democratic free America.

1) As a people united, we will no longer tolerate corruption and fraud in the office of the President of the United States.
2) As a people united, we will no longer tolerate corruption and fraud in the federal, state and local political offices.
3) As a people united, we will no longer tolerate corruption and fraud in law enforcement offices.
4) As a people united, we will no longer tolerate suppression of freedom of speech by government or private corporations.
5) As a people united, we will no longer tolerate presidential, federal, political, corporate and law enforcement abuse of power.

6) As a people united, we will no longer tolerate totalitarian tactics enacted by government, law enforcement agencies or private corporations.

7) As a people united, we will no longer tolerate police state tactics enacted by government, law enforcement agencies or private corporations.

8) As a people united, we will no longer tolerate martial law enacted permanently by government, and law enforcement agencies.

9) As a people united, we will no longer tolerate curfews permanently imposed by government and law enforcement agencies.

10) As a people united, we will no longer tolerate taxation without first democratic representation presented to the people.

11) As a people united, we will no longer tolerate careless spending of taxpayers dollars by government.

12) As a people united, we will no longer tolerate unfair tax loopholes utilized by private corporations that. shift greater tax burdens on the middleclass and poor.

13) As a people united, we will no longer tolerate experimentation on the people, society, and the environment by government, military, or private corporation without first democratic representation to the people.

14) As a people united, we will no longer tolerate development and use of any product or service by private corporation or government that knowingly compromises the safety of the people, society or the environment.

15) As a people united, we will not tolerate corporate and government non-adherence to federal, state, and local laws.

16) As a people united, we will no longer tolerate unethical, destructive exploitation of society, commerce, American workers, American consumers and the environment by private corporations and government for greed, profit, and personal gain.

17) As a people united, we will no longer tolerate apathy and incompetence on behalf of the government toward corporate and political crimes.

18) As a people united, we will no longer tolerate violation of labor laws, consumer laws, safety laws, and environmental protection laws by government and private corporations.

19) As a people united, we will no longer tolerate corruption, fraud, apathy, and incompetence on behalf of government agencies created to protect labor laws, consumer laws, safety laws, and environmental protection laws.

20) As a people united, we will no longer tolerate substandard wages, declining wages, benefits and declining quality of life imposed on American workers as a direct result of excessive corporate greed, exploitation and profiteering.

21) As a people united, we will no longer tolerate unsafe, unethical work conditions forced unwillingly upon American workers.

22) As a people united, we will no longer tolerate the exporting of sound, stable American jobs to foreign countries leaving American workers unemployed, or underpaid.

23) As a people united, we will no longer tolerate early release program for violent criminals.

24) As a people united, we will no longer tolerate crime severity reduction, crime record deletion practices, or other forms of apathy by cities and law enforcement agencies to intentionally reduce crime percentages.

25) As a people united, we will no longer tolerate racial, religious, sexual, age, or handicapped discrimination by government and private corporations.

26) As a people united, we will no longer tolerate refusal to treat any life threatening injury or illness by medical care facilities because of patient's inability to pay or lack of insurance.

27) As a people united, we will no longer tolerate apathy or disrespect toward any veteran of war, veteran of law enforcement, or any causes, illnesses relating.

28) As a people united, we will no longer tolerate additions, alterations, deletions, or any attempts to repress or neutralize articles of the Constitution of the United States of America without first democratic process presented to the people in a

manner, language easily understandable to the average citizen, and free of deception and fraud.

29) As a People united, we will no longer tolerate deception and fraud by government, political leaders, law enforcement, or corporate America to gain public support, votes or legislation for any reason what so ever.

30) To ensure adherence to the plans, visions, and dreams set forth and bestowed upon the American people by the founding fathers, and to prevent further decay of democratic principles, processes, freedom of choice, American prosperity, and American middleclass, we the people united will no longer tolerate social and economic oppression of democratic free America by government or corporate America.

The government and it's elected officials are hereby presented with this formal ultimatum and are to answer only to the American people united exercising their Constitutional rights bestowed upon them by the founding fathers of America, or said government will be dissolved by democratic process as directed by the founding fathers and replaced with new government created by the people for the people honoring the Declaration of Independence, Bill of Rights and the Constitution of the United States on this_____day of _____the year_____.

Sincerely_____

name_____
street_____
city, state, zip_____

About Jay T. Baldwin

I am a typical American blue collar worker. I am the youngest with a brother and a sister, we were born to a middleclass family in the suburbs of Maryland. We were raised very comfortable but not spoiled in a one income household, with mom home to raise us. Not quite the Brady Bunch!, but a typical American family in the late 50's and early 60's.

Today I am married to my wife Zenaida, and we currently have one beautiful child named Adriana. We plan on having more children in the future. Being a working husband and father has made me realize the importance of maintaining a functional middle-class standard of living.

Working full time jobs in the 80's, we were self sufficient and savored the American Dream through hard stable work. With one income household, we lived the quality of life of our parents with one income households in the 50's and 60's did. However, since the early 1990's, we have watched our middleclass standard of living slowly slide into the poverty zone. Now with two incomes, we can not live the quality of life we were used to, much less the quality of life our parents did with one income three decades ago. I even learned two alternative trades in a vain effort to evade declining wages. Now with experience and training in three different trades and my wife's job, our gross earnings have dropped from a comfortable $28,000 a year to about $13,000. Now even with two incomes, and the fact the cost of living has almost doubled since the 1980's we are at poverty level and literally dependent on our parents again.

According to my research on this trend, I feel this downward mobility of our family and the American people will continue past the year 2000. As personal experiences from our combined families, and the observations of our friends, co-workers, and peer groups, I see this same story being repeated across the nation. I am now virtually incapable of supporting our family on today's meager wages. We once had the American Dream, however, now it's just a faded memory!